ABOUT CANADA
IMMIGRATION

ABOUT CANADA
IMMIGRATION

Nupur Gogia & Bonnie Slade

About Canada Series

Fernwood Publishing • Halifax & Winnipeg

Copyright © 2011 Nupur Gogia and Bonnie Slade

All rights reserved. No part of this book may be reproduced or transmitted in any form by any means without permission in writing from the publisher, except by a reviewer, who may quote brief passages in a review.

Editing and design: Brenda Conroy
Cover design: John van der Woude
Printed and bound in Canada by Hignell Book Printing

Published in Canada by Fernwood Publishing
32 Oceanvista Lane, Black Point, Nova Scotia, B0J 1B0
and 748 Broadway Avenue, Winnipeg, MB R3G 0X3
www.fernwoodpublishing.ca

Fernwood Publishing Company Limited gratefully acknowledges the financial support of the Government of Canada through the Canada Book Fund, the Canada Council for the Arts, the Nova Scotia Department of Tourism and Culture and the Province of Manitoba, through the Book Publishing Tax Credit, for our publishing program.

Library and Archives Canada Cataloguing in Publication

Gogia, Nupur
Immigration / Nupur Gogia, Bonnie Slade.

(About Canada)
Includes bibliographical references.
ISBN 978-1-55266-407-0 (pbk.).–ISBN 978-1-55266-431-5 (bound)

 1. Canada–Emigration and immigration–Government
policy–History. 2. Immigrants–Canada–Economic
conditions–21st century. I. Slade, Bonnie, 1964- II. Title.
III. Series: About Canada series

JV7233.N86 2011   305.9'069120971   C2010-908041-6

CONTENTS

INTRODUCTION – IMMIGRATION: A CRITICAL ANALYSIS 7
    Migration 8
    Myths about Immigration 10
    Theories of Migration 11
    How This Book Is Organized 13

1. THE EVOLUTION OF IMMIGRATION POLICY: LEARNING ABOUT THE PAST TO UNDERSTAND THE PRESENT 15
    Constructing a White Nation, 1869–1967 19
    The Door Opens, 1967–present 29
    Conclusion 33

2. IMMIGRATION POLICY AND PRACTICES: THE MECHANICS OF MIGRATION 34
    The Current System 37
    Economic Class 39
    Family Class 47
    Refugees 50
    Critiques of Immigration Policy 53
    Summary 56

3. IMMIGRANTS AND THE LABOUR MARKET: DEVALUATION, FRUSTRATION AND DOWNWARD MOBILITY 58
    Key Reports 64
    Devaluation of Credentials, Experience and Networks 66
    Impact of the Underemployment of Immigrants 71

4. THE RECEPTION PARTY: THE SETTLEMENT PROCESS FOR IMMIGRANTS ... 74

What Is Settlement?..76
Addressing Settlement Issues...80
How Settlement Services Work 82
Is Settlement Working?..84
Conclusion...87

5. THE REVOLVING DOOR: TEMPORARY WORKERS IN CANADA......................88

History of Temporary Foreign Workers in Canada 90
Temporary Foreign Workers Today 93
Case Study 1: The Mexican Seasonal Agricultural Worker Program 97
Case Study 2: The Untold Tale of Local Food...99
Conclusion...102

6. UNDER THE SURFACE: CANADA'S HIDDEN LABOUR FORCE.....................103

Lifestyles of the Invisible and Non-Status...105
Myths and Realities..106
Here to Stay — The Systemic Reality of Non-Status Immigrants 109
Government and Community Responses to Non-Status Immigrants 110
Conclusion...116

7. COMING TO A BETTER PLACE?: NOT ALWAYS A HAPPY ENDING 118

Land of Opportunity or Depot of Dumped Labour?...121

ENDNOTES...124

RESOURCES 132

APPENDIX 1: TOP SOURCE COUNTRIES OF IMMIGRANTS 1968–2008..........136

APPENDIX 2: FEDERAL SKILLED WORKER ASSESSMENT TEST......................138

ACKNOWLEDGEMENTS..143

ABOUT CANADA..144

Introduction

IMMIGRATION
A Critical Analysis

"Canada is a land of immigrants." What does this oft repeated phrase mean? The answer seems clear enough — Canada was built by and is made up of people of many different races, nationalities, cultures and languages. However, this cozy pluralistic notion hides many complicated realities of both the history of immigration and the experience of coming to Canada as an immigrant today. On the surface migration appears to be a straightforward process. People move, either by choice or displacement, from one country to another. Each country sets its own criteria, or immigration policy, for people entering to settle permanently or to work temporarily. For the migrant, the move can be risky and may represent opportunity, may embody hope and fear. For the receiving country, the influx of new people may be beneficial economically, socially and culturally. But immigration raises a complex web of political and social issues that are mired in a country's specific history, values and hierarchies. For Canada, the motives for encouraging immigration include ensuring population and economic growth and preserving territorial boundaries. These motives change over time, as Canada shifts its own internal priorities and its place on a global stage.

There continues to be a perception that Canada's laws make it easy for immigrants to come here and that Canada is more welcoming and hospitable to new immigrants than many other countries. The perceptions, however, are not always true or true for everyone. This book critically examines these perceptions and investigates the history of how and which immigrants contributed to the making of Canada. We do not take as a given that all immigrants' lives are enhanced in Canada. Like some early immigrants who left middle-class and privileged lives for the hardship of pioneer life in Canada, many immigrants who come to Canada today do not experience an improvement in their lives. Furthermore, the selection of who gets to come to Canada, while no longer explicitly based on race (as was historically the case), is still predicated on a certain class of immigrants, who often discover that neither their education nor their work experience allows them to continue their profession or occupation. In addition to these issues, this book explores pressing issues such as temporary labour programs, labour market integration issues, including lack of skills' recognition and undocumented labour, and the role of the state in welcoming and integrating new citizens.

Migration

Migration is a global phenomenon, and there are more people on the move today than ever before. The reasons include economic displacement, family reunification, environmental degradation, war and civil unrest and sometimes, quite simply, the search for a better life. The International Organization for Migration estimates that there are approximately 214 million international migrants in the world today, which is about 3.1 percent of the global population. This number of migrants would equal the fifth most populous country in the world. Contrary to the myth that it is primarily men who migrate, 49 percent of international migrants are women.[1]

As a receiving country for migrants, Canada falls right in the middle of the top ten, hosting approximately 7.2 million migrants in 2008 (see Table 0.1). The top country to host immigrants is the

Table 0.1 Top Ten Countries Hosting International Migrants, 2008

Country	Number of Migrants (millions)
United States	42.8
Russian Federation	12.3
Germany	10.8
Saudi Arabia	7.3
Canada	7.2
France	6.7
United Kingdom	6.5
Spain	6.4
India	5.4
Ukraine	5.3

Source: International Organization for Migration, "World Migration 2008: Managing Labour Mobility in the Evolving Global Economy: Regional and Country Figures," at <iom.int/jahia/Jahia/about-migration/facts-and-figures/regional-and-country-figures>. (n.d.).

United States (42.8 million), followed by the Russian Federation, Germany and Saudi Arabia. While Canada may not be the first country of choice for international migrants, we do have a larger proportion of immigrants (21.6 percent) in our general population than either the United States (13.8 percent) or the Russian Federation (8.7 percent). The top three migrant-sending countries are China (35 million), India (20 million) and the Philippines (7 million).[2] Many global migration trends run counter to the myths we commonly associate with immigration. For example, the majority of African migrants move within Africa, while Asia, the largest source of temporary workers, is also characterized by large flows of intra-regional migration, particularly in China and India. The Middle East is the most important destination for temporary Asian workers, and temporary migrant labour is on the rise in Europe, the United States and Canada. In the case of Canada, the number of migrants coming through temporary worker channels has lately exceeded those coming through the permanent residency category.

Myths about Immigration

There exists a plethora of myths about immigration. Before exploring some of the more complex issues surrounding immigration, we discuss and debunk some of the most often cited beliefs around immigrants and immigration to Canada.

It Is Easy to Immigrate to Canada

Canada's point system makes it very difficult except for the most highly skilled and highly educated people to achieve enough points to even be considered for immigration. In fact, it is estimated that many Canadians would not pass the point system test if it was applied to them.

Immigrants Steal Jobs from Canadian Workers

Although the majority of immigrants who come to Canada as permanent residents are highly skilled professionals, their qualifications are frequently not recognized. Consequently, they are not able to compete with Canadians for jobs in their field. In fact, it is estimated that new immigrants are three times more likely to be working in low-skilled jobs than their Canadian counterparts. Furthermore, between 1993 and 2001, even semi-established immigrants (those who had been in the country for ten years or less) had higher rates of overqualification than Canadians doing similar work.[3]

Immigrants are Destitute, Uneducated and a Drain on the System

Canada's immigration system is designed to bring in more Skilled Workers than any other category of immigrants. Most immigrants come to Canada with advanced degrees, professional status and a high level of experience, all of which contributes to giving Canada an edge in the competitive global market. Immigrants who come to Canada as business migrants are required to have a minimum net worth of $800,000! Upon settling in Canada, they establish businesses and create new jobs for Canadians. Regardless of the channel of immigration, whether it be Economic or Family Class, immigrants are required to bring a certain amount of money to ensure that they will not be dependant on Canada's social security system.

Immigrants Bring Crime to Canada
Immigrants actually have lower crime rates than the Canadian-born population, and according to the International Centre for Criminal Law Reform and Criminal Justice Policy, immigrants are "much less involved in criminal activity than are those who were born in Canada."[4]

Immigrants Do Not Want to Work
Most immigrants come to Canada because they seek a better life for themselves and their children. As part of that new life, most immigrants hope to find suitable and fulfilling work. However, for many immigrants, finding a decent job is frequently more challenging than they anticipated. Many immigrants who are doctors and engineers end up working as drivers, cleaners and security agents because they cannot land a job in their field.

Theories of Migration

There are numerous theories about why people migrate. On the face of it, most people move because they want a better life. While this reason for migration is almost always true, there are often other more complex factors at work that compel people to uproot themselves and their families from their jobs, homes, friends and families in order to attempt a new life somewhere else. Some of these factors may involve individual experiences (i.e., loss of land, death in the family), while others may be more structural (i.e., civil unrest, economic downturn). Whatever the reason, the reality is that migration is almost never an easy decision or process.

There are two approaches to looking at migration — the individual and the structural. The individual approach, also known as "human capital theory," argues that individuals will rationally assess which country is offering the best employment and wage prospects for their skills and experience and make their decisions accordingly. The limitation to this approach is that migration decisions are rarely made by lone individuals who simply evaluate money and jobs. Migration decisions are frequently influenced by other family members, contacts individuals have in other countries, the desirability of locating to other countries, and a host of other factors.

Another way of looking at migration is the structural approach, which is also referred to as "push-pull theory." This theory at its most simple argues that there are factors, such as poverty, unemployment and conflict (to name just a few), that push people out of their countries, and other factors, such as jobs, economic prosperity and political stability, that pull those same people into other countries. There are a number of variations on this theory as well. For example, the "dual or segmented labour market theory" asserts that a capitalist system will create two levels of employment — high-skilled and low-skilled. High-skilled employment consists of jobs that are well-paid, secure and offer job protection and benefits. Low-skilled employment, also known as the three-D jobs — dirty, dangerous and difficult — are frequently difficult to fill because most locals are not interested in working under those conditions. Thus, countries often import immigrants to work in low-skilled jobs, often found in the construction, agriculture and service industries. A second variation of the push-pull theory is the "neoclassical economic theory," which argues that international migration is connected to the global supply and demand for labour. In this theory, migrants from countries with surplus labour are attracted to the potential for high wages and good jobs in countries that are experiencing labour shortages. Lastly, the "world systems theory" posits that international migration is a consequence of global capitalism. The industrial development of rich nations (the pull countries) has created structural economic problems in poor countries (the push countries), resulting in the large-scale international migration of people from the "Third World" to the "First World."[5]

How This Book Is Organized

The book contains seven chapters, with Chapter 1 examining how Canadian immigration policy from 1867 to 1967 was explicitly formulated with the goal of creating and maintaining a white settler society. This chapter also explores immigration policies since 1967, after the elimination of race-based criteria, and discusses whether racial discrimination has been eliminated. Chapter 2 outlines current immigration policy and explains how it works. It analyzes the shifts in immigration policy, noting the devolution of federal government control of the process and the increasing involvement of other actors such as post-secondary institutions, provincial governments and employers. While the policies are no longer based on race, they are still highly selective, favouring middle-class professionals.

Chapter 3 addresses labour issues for immigrant professionals and skilled workers. As immigration trends have shifted with respect to source countries and annual quotas, professionals are experiencing greater difficulties in establishing themselves in their professions than immigrants of the past. Chapter 4 deals with integration issues ranging from language training to accessing culturally appropriate health and social services. For the most recent wave of immigrants, many of whom come from the Global South, integrating into Canadian society is a challenging process fraught with many obstacles including poverty and social isolation. This chapter investigates the framework of settlement services in Canada and whether these foster the social inclusion of new immigrants or exacerbate their social exclusion.

Chapter 5 discusses the dramatic growth in the numbers of temporary workers and work programs in the past five years. Following on the heels of both Europe and the United States, Canada is witnessing an explosion in temporary worker programs. These programs import migrants, typically from countries in the Global South, to perform labour for a specified period. Upon completion of this period, migrants are sent back to their countries of origin. Temporary labour programs are designed to meet the labour needs in industries where there is a shortage of Canadians workers. Lauded as a panacea for both Canadian industry and poor workers from the South, Canadian temporary labour programs are being heralded across the globe. But who really benefits from these programs? Are structural inequalities in these programs ushering in a new form of "slave" labour? This chapter highlights the Seasonal Agricultural Migrant Worker Program to examine how temporary labour programs in Canada are creating a new underclass of labourers.

Non-status migrants is the theme of Chapter 6. Performing invisible labour — from cleaning offices to constructing basements — Canada's estimated 200,000 undocumented workers form an integral yet hidden part of the national workforce. For example, the construction industry in Ontario employs over 76,000 illegal workers. This chapter explores the rise of undocumented labour in Canada and contemporary debates surrounding this sector of workers.

The final chapter argues that there is a need for federal, provincial and municipal levels of government to work together to improve the outcomes of immigration for both the individuals who migrate and for the communities in which they live. The under and unemployment of immigrants in Canada is the result of systemic policies and practices, such as not recognizing international credentials and work experience as equivalent to Canadian, and they can be changed. Immigrants deserve to be treated with more respect in Canada. The aim of this book is to contribute to making much needed changes to immigration policies and practices, employer hiring practices and Canadians' attitudes towards immigrants.

1. THE EVOLUTION OF IMMIGRATION POLICY
Learning about the Past to Understand the Present

> The story of Canadian immigration is not one of orderly population growth; it has been and remains both a catalyst to Canadian economic development and a mirror of Canadian attitudes and values; it has often been unashamedly and economically self-serving and ethnically or racially biased.[1]

Immigration is a constantly changing process. By examining how immigration policy has changed over time, it is possible to see how the prevailing ideas about Canada and Canadian identity also shift, and are challenged and resisted. The above assessment by the *Canadian Encyclopedia* is supported by numerous examples of racial and ethnic discrimination. The following are a couple of many:

> One of the major migrations to Canada occurred after the American War of Independence (1775–1783). Many people living in America remained loyal to Britain, fought against the Americans, and moved north to Canada when America ceased to be an British colony at the end of the war. Over 90,000 of these migrants, called United Empire Loyalists, relocated to Upper and Lower Canada and the Atlantic Provinces. Of this diverse group, which included Aboriginal people and European migrants, approximately 10 percent were Black

Loyalists, African Americans who had been promised their freedom in exchange for their loyalty. For their contribution to the war effort, all Loyalists were granted land in Canada, often in two-hundred-acre allotments. Black Loyalists, however, experienced much longer processing times for land grant claims than white Loyalists, received less land and were given land in harsher, harder to cultivate areas. Many Black Loyalists eventually emigrated from Canada to Sierra Leone to escape the hardships and unequal treatment.

Despite Canada's image and government rhetoric of being a safe harbour for people fleeing persecution, Canada had the worst record of any country, accepting only 4,000 to 5,000 Jewish refugees between 1933 and 1945. The groundbreaking book by Irving Abella and Harold Troper, *None Is Too Many*,[2] details how the Canadian government used administrative practices to limit the number of Jewish migrants and refugees to Canada. Despite the context of the Holocaust, in which Jews were being imprisoned and murdered by the Nazis, Canadian politicians continued to close the door on European Jews. After the war, it was easier for Nazi war criminals to immigrate to Canada than it was for Jews.

Students of Canadian immigration are often surprised by what they learn. Although it is often said that Canada is a nation of immigrants, for many whose ancestors immigrated to Canada several generations ago, their family stories of migration may be long forgotten. As a result many people lose the awareness that *all* non-Aboriginal Canadians have a migration story in their past. This loss of personal history is almost exclusively only true for "white" people of British or French ancestry. For people whose families have moved to Canada in their lifetime and for people from racialized communities whose families have been in Canada for many generations, however, the issue of immigration is very prominent in their lives. They are constantly faced with questions of belonging, are assumed by many Canadians to be outsiders and are often reminded that they have a story of migration to Canada.

One of the goals of this book is to help readers to develop a curiosity about the past and to make the connection between current and past events. When Bonnie Slade was growing up she had no knowledge of her family history. Through genealogical research she discovered that her ancestry traces back to James Grey, a United Empire Loyalist who settled in Prince Edward County (Ontario) in the 1780s, and to the Boudrain family, who moved to Île d'Orléans from Normandy, France, in the 1680s. Despite these deep roots in Canada, she had no sense of the stories of how her ancestors had made their way to Canada, the hardships they surely endured and their experiences of integrating into this emerging country. Thus, her lineage extends back to the appropriation of First Nations land by European governments in their quest for colonial expansion, first by the French government in their building of New France and second by the British Crown. Her story is representative of many other multigenerational white Canadians with British ancestry who have lost touch with and therefore stopped telling their stories of migration. Even Canadians who feel a sense of always having been here have a story of migration that has been forgotten. By losing the knowledge of our family stories of migration we lose touch with an important piece of our history and the history of Canada.

We start this book with a chapter on history because of our conviction that knowledge of the past is critical to an understanding of the present. The importance of knowing history was stressed by the Spanish philosopher George Santayana,[3] who wrote, "those who cannot remember the past are condemned to repeat it." As you read through this chapter, try and see the linkages between immigration policy and practices of the past and those of the current day.

Most accounts of Canadian immigration history focus on formal immigration policy and the relationship between French and English settlers. In this book we add our voices to a growing chorus arguing that a broader perspective is needed to fully understand the development of Canada. Immigration policy and practices need to be viewed alongside domestic policies of nation-building, which simultaneously and systematically excluded certain groups of people from citizenship rights such as voting, freedom of movement and employment. For example, in 1876, after numerous signed treaties and agreements with Aboriginal peoples were broken by the Canadian government, the *Indian Act* was passed to control First Nations peoples through such measures as reserves and residential schools. Thus, we need to view Canada as a country based on the displacement of the indigenous peoples, alongside the intentional recruitment of white English and European peoples to create a specific population and cultural traditions. This is our history.

In this chapter we trace immigration history over two broad periods, chosen on the basis of immigration criteria and selection practices. While European, American, African and Asian people had been migrating to Canada for three centuries prior, the first formalized immigration policy in Canada was not enacted until 1869. The first period we examine includes the almost one hundred years from 1869 to 1967; the second is from 1967 to the present. Until 1967, when the point system was introduced, the Canadian government overtly used race as a criterion for immigrant selection. Prior to the point system, immigration applicants were treated differently based on their race and nationality, divided into "desirable" and "undesirable" migrants, who were subject to differing administrative procedures and requirements, some being outright barred from entering Canada. Drawing on primary historical sources such as newspaper and magazine articles, this chapter provides an overview of immigration history, highlighting several key moments to illustrate how the state used immigration policy and practice to construct a nation comprised of particular people. Questions this chapter addresses include: Who was considered to be an ideal citizen and who was deemed a threat to the national identity? What steps did governments take to encourage migration from England and Europe and to discourage migration from Asia and Southeast Asia? How does the legacy of race-based immigration policies and practices linger in Canada today? It is worthwhile to think about your own family story of migration as you read this history. How does your family's migration story fit into the history of Canada?

Constructing a White Nation, 1869–1967

> It is one of our great national myths that Canada has a long history of welcoming refugees and dissidents, of always being in the forefront of accepting the world's oppressed and dispossessed, of being receptive and hospitable to wave after wave of immigrants… yet as the recent literature in Canadian history has shown, the Canadian record is one of which we ought not to be proud. Our treatment of our native people as well as our abysmal history in admitting blacks, Chinese, Japanese, Indians and during 1930s and 1940s Jews, should lay to rest the myth of our liberalism and enlightenment on matters of race and immigration.[4]

In 1867, the year of Confederation, Canada was comprised of Nova Scotia, New Brunswick, Southern Quebec and Southern Ontario — a much different geographic entity than it is now. With a population in Canada of 3,565,000 in 1869, the Canadian government passed its first *Immigration Act*. Dealing mainly with issues of public health and quarantine, the Act did not initially set any restrictions on who could enter Canada. The vast majority of immigrants were then coming from Britain and the United States, but some migrants from Europe, Africa, Asia and Southeast Asia also came to Canada in search of work and opportunity.

In the expansion of Canada from coast to coast to coast, there was a need for labourers to perform all sorts of work. When British Columbia joined Canada in 1871, a plan was set to build a national railroad by 1885 that would span the entire country. This ambitious goal required workers, and from 1881 to 1885, Canada recruited more than 15,000 Chinese men to work on the construction of the Canadian railroad:

> The building of the Canadian Pacific and Canadian National Railways called for skilled professionals. It called for surveyors and engineers who could plan the routes and the grades, experts who could choose the locomotives and rolling stock suited to Canadian conditions, as well as managers who could oversee the complex operations. Then there were people who carried out the orders—thousands of Irish and Chinese labourers were brought into the country for the back-breaking manual work.[5]

When the railroad was completed in 1885 and the need for mass cheap labour was over, the government levied a $50 head tax on Chinese immigrants. The *Chinese Immigration Act*, the first formal race-based immigration restriction, sought to preserve the British and white character of Canada by discouraging further immigration from China. Even within this hostile environment many Chinese stayed in British Columbia, working in the forests, mines and factories. When it became obvious that the head tax was not stopping Chinese immigration, it was increased to $100 in 1899, and to $500 in 1903. At the time, $500 represented two years of wages for a Chinese labourer, and today it is equivalent to over $55,000. These fees slowed the flow of labourers from China and also acted as a barrier to family reunification. Chinese women were not wanted in Canada as they were seen to be the key to the development of permanent Chinese communities. The impact of this gender-based exclusion was severe; for example, in Alberta in the late 1930s, there were 305 Chinese women compared to 2,817 Chinese men. In addition to the exorbitant immigration fees, various jurisdictions used other means to dissuade Chinese migration. For example, Chinese Canadians were forbidden from acquiring Crown Land in British Columbia in the early 1900s. Also, from 1904 to 1907, the Province of British Columbia tried to restrict non-white immigrants from Asia by not allowing them to vote, serve on juries or work in the professions.

As the project of settling the Prairies and Western Canada was unfolding in the late 1800s and early 1900s, the government used notions of suitability to exclude Black farmers who were relocating from the United States, escaping from the post Civil War racism. The reception they received in Canada was chilly, especially when settling in emerging rural communities comprised mostly of white settlers in what was being constructed as a white nation. Meanwhile the Aboriginal and Métis population in these provinces was relocated to reserves and controlled through the *Indian Act*. Although this was never an explicit government policy, Black farmers were often deemed unsuitable for the Canadian climate by immigration officials. They faced lengthy interviews and medical examinations by border guards, and when no good excuse could be found to deny them entry, a $50 entrance fee was imposed. By using such administrative tools, the government prevented many Blacks from migrating to Canada.

This race-based immigration exclusion was intensified against the Chinese and broadened to include the Japanese and South Asians. Restrictions were extended to Japanese migrants, although this was undertaken as a "gentlemen's agreement" between the Canadian and Japanese governments and was not formally written into immigration regulations. The agreement, developed in 1907 after an anti-Chinese and anti-Japanese race riot in Vancouver, outlined that Japan would allow no more than four hundred male migrants each year to apply for immigration to Canada. The number of women was also restricted, given that Japanese women were travelling to Canada as brides for Japanese men. These women faced great hardship; in addition to being a wife and working in the home, many women also worked in mines and factories, earning money for the family.

In addition to targeting Chinese and Japanese migrants, the

Canadian government attempted to limit both male and female migration from South Asia. The *Continuous Passage Act*, enacted in 1908 and effective until 1947, stated that all immigrants were required to travel to Canada by continuous passage from their country of origin or citizenship on a through-ticket purchased in that country. Since no shipping company provided direct service from either South Asia or Southeast Asia to Canada, this effectively placed a ban on immigration from these areas.

The *Continuous Passage Act* was challenged directly by a group of Sikhs, Hindus and Muslims. Setting out on the *Komagata Maru* from Hong Kong, the 376 passengers, all British citizens, arrived in Vancouver on May 23, 1914, and demanded entry into Canada. The Canadian government refused to let them land, and the passengers were forced to stay on board the ship. The South Asian community in Canada rallied around the plight of the passengers, providing supplies and lawyers to plead their case. While the government was trying to turn these 376 people away, immigration was robust. In 1913, Canada admitted 400,870 immigrants, the highest number of immigrants admitted in a single year in the history of Canada. In 1913, immigrant arrivals made up 5.3 percent of Canada's population, far exceeding contemporary attempts to recruit 1 percent annually. It was in this climate of intense immigration that Canadian authorities stated, "Hindus would never be allowed to land in Canada," revealing the deeply held racist views and race-based foundation to the immigration system. Canada did not just want immigrants, it wanted white immigrants from Britain or Europe.

On July 23, 1914, after two months of negotiation, twenty-four passengers were allowed to land and the other 352 were forced to leave Canada without ever disembarking from the ship. An official apology was given by the Province of British Columbia on the seventy-fifth anniversary of the landing of the *Komagata Maru*.[6]

The story of the *Komagata Maru* and its passengers ended even more tragically. When the ship returned to Calcutta, the passengers were immediately arrested by the British and the boat was diverted to Budge Budge, a port seventeen miles away. They learned that they were going to be sent to Punjab on a train. Since most of the passengers wanted to stop in Calcutta, not Punjab, they decided to march back. Their march was short-lived, however, and they were forced back to the boat by police. When they were ordered to get back on the boat, a skirmish broke out, the British police opened fire and twenty passengers were killed.

An interesting contrast to the *Komagata Maru* incident that illustrates how Canadian officials treated immigrants differently according to their race and gender can be seen in the Female Assisted Passage programs, which took place in the 1860s in Victoria. Between 1859 and 1870, approximately 130 white, working-class women from England were recruited to Victoria to work as domestics and to eventually marry local men. The importation of white women was a specific strategy to establish Victoria as a white settler society, for up to this point in time white women formed only between 5 and 35 percent of the white population in Victoria. While the *Komagata Maru* drew crowds of suspicious and scornful Vancouver residents, the ships bringing the "fair" women to Victoria were met by crowds of hundreds of men, leering, wanting to meet the women.[7]

In the early 1910s, blatant and widespread racism toward Chinese immigrants intensified. In an attempt to "stop the evils of Oriental immigration,"[8] a plan was set in place to photograph all Chinese people in Canada to assist in crime control. Such racism against Chinese people was publicly acceptable; this plan was described in a front-page article in the *Toronto Daily News* on January 24, 1913:

> The average Anglo-Saxon is incapable of distinguishing with any degree of certainty different members of the Chinese race. He only knows that the man before him is a Chinaman, with the characteristic eyes, features, pigmentation and gibberish of the Oriental. The difficulty is only increased by the Chinaman's

notorious disregard of the truth, and low estimate of his oath. Photographs and body marks should assist greatly in the identification of Chinese criminals and in the administration of justice to these, the most elusive of wrongdoers.

From 1885 and 1923, it is estimated by the Chinese Canadian National Council that $23 million in head taxes was collected by the federal government. In 1923, the *Chinese Immigration Act* (also known as the *Chinese Exclusion Act*) was passed, formally excluding all Chinese people from immigrating to Canada. Between 1923 and 1947, when this Act was repealed, only eight wealthy immigrants from China were admitted, in an attempt to procure trade for Canada. [9] Again it took the government some time to recognize the injustice. It was not until June 22, 2006, that the prime minister offered an apology to the Chinese community and compensation for those who were subjected to these discriminatory laws. The government offered $20,000 directly to survivors or their spouses, but not their children. Because the head tax was levied so many years ago, there were few survivors to collect the compensation money.

Chinese, Japanese and South Asian immigration was successfully restricted through regulations, which did not require formal legislation or legislative approval. Regulations were also used to encourage immigration from countries considered to be "desirable," such as England. In 1923, the very same year the *Chinese Exclusion Act* was passed, the federal government created measures to increase the number of British immigrants by offering transportation assistance and other enticements. A hundred government agents were hired and stationed in Britain and were paid a $2 bonus for each British agricultural labourer recruited and placed in Ontario or Quebec.[10]

While in many cases it was men who first moved to Canada to work as labourers, followed later by his wife, fiancée or family, many women also travelled to Canada as labourers. Domestic work, in particular, was felt to be the domain of women, and Britain was the preferred source for domestic workers. Between 1904 and 1914,

16,000 women emigrated to Canada as domestic workers, 12,000 of whom were from Britain.[11] The recruitment of domestic workers from Britain became institutionalized in the federal government after World War I in a special division of the Department of Immigration and Colonization. This department was responsible not only for identifying appropriate British women for domestic work but also for monitoring them in their work places.

Additional schemes were undertaken by the federal government in the 1920s to stimulate immigration from Britain. In 1928, the cost of transportation from the British Isles to Canada was reduced from $95 to $50. Reduced rates and free passage were offered to land settlers and female household workers. In rural Ontario, a hundred cottages were built for British settlers, with the $1,000 cost shared between the British, Canadian and provincial governments. From 1928 until 1930, there was a program for British boys between the ages of fourteen and nineteen to live and apprentice on farms in Ontario, Manitoba or New Brunswick. When the youth were twenty-one years old, they were granted a loan to set up their own farm. According to an article in *Saturday Night*: "With all the provinces eventually co-operating, the program should mean a considerable advance in the effort to enlarge the population and maintain the British ratio."[12]

In 1930, in the context of an economic depression, immigration levels were significantly reduced and the decision-making power for immigration, including the authority to "exclude immigrants belonging to any race deemed unsuited to the climate or requirements of Canada," was decentralized to the provinces:

> The whole responsibility of deciding how many new settlers shall come to Canada each year, their sex, age, race and character — agricultural worker or white-collar men — is to be placed upon the Provinces. The Dominion will undertake to find the kind and numbers of immigrants desired by each Province and will continue to shoulder all burdens of deporta-

tion, thus assuring that the Provinces will not be saddled with the expense of keeping misfits.[13]

Indeed deportation of "undesirable" immigrants was a serious project. Between 1930 and 1935, approximately 30,000 people were deported, and while most of these were of European descent, it was predominantly working-class people who were deported for economic reasons. These deportations occurred during the Great Depression, a period of harsh economic times for all Canadians. By deporting poor European immigrants and political activists the government sought to avoid or reduce economic and social unrest.

At the end of the World War II, Canada was the world's fifth largest industrial power. Because of the need for skilled workers in the decade-long economic boom of 1947 to 1957, immigration restrictions were gradually removed. In 1947, the *Chinese Exclusion Act* and the *Continuous Passage Act* were both repealed; the goal of maintaining a white settler society, however, remained intact. During the introduction of the immigration changes, Prime Minister MacKenzie King stated:

> People of Canada do not wish as a result of mass immigration to make a fundamental alteration in the character of our population. Large-scale immigration from the Orient would change the fundamental composition of the Canadian population.[14]

Immigration from Britain, the United States and northern European countries continued to be preferred; immigration from China and India was still restricted. The prime minister assured the population that "the government has no intention of removing existing regulations respecting Asiatic immigration unless and until alternative measures of control have been worked out."[15] The prime minister's position reflected public opinion. According to Harold Troper:

> Just over a year after the guns fell quiet in Europe, a public opinion poll found that Canadians would rather see recently defeated Germans allowed into Canada than Eastern and

THE EVOLUTION OF IMMIGRATION POLICY

Southern Europeans, and Jews in particular. Only the Japanese fared worse. Thus, even a grudging willingness to reopen immigration in late 1947 was very much predicated on holding to the ethnically and racially based immigration priorities of the 1920s.[16]

Although immigrants who arrived in Canada during the early 1950s brought with them a great diversity of skills, they were almost all from Europe. This influx of skills was crucial to Canada's economic development as immigration accounted for almost 50 percent of the labour force increase between 1950 and 1960, and 65 percent of the increase from 1950 to 1955. Between 1954 and 1967, 83 percent of immigrants were from Europe, 4 percent from Asia and 1 percent from Africa. The door was opening, but very slowly.

The 1957 Royal Commission on Canada's Economic Prospects identified the shortage of skilled workers as a major problem. In the 1950s, the majority of Canadians over the age of fifteen had less than a grade nine education.[17] Canada benefited immensely during the 1950s and 1960s from the integration of immigrant professionals into the Canadian labour market both by gaining their experience and by not having to fund their education. It is important to note that race, class and gender intersected in particular ways such that white European professionals were accepted and encouraged to contribute to Canadian society while non-white, non-European immigrants faced labour market barriers. As we show in Chapter 3, racialized immigrant professionals continue to face enormous barriers to re-establishing their careers in Canada.

Globally, post World War II, nations and international bodies such as the United Nations developed policies to address social inequality. In 1948, the United Nations adopted the *Universal Declaration of Human Rights*, and in 1951 the Office of the United Nations High Commissioner for Refugees ratified the *Convention Relating to the Status of Refugees*. Canada participated in and was impacted by these global actions. The *Canadian Bill of Rights* was enacted in 1960, making discrimination based on race, colour, national origin, religion or gender illegal. The *Immigration Act* was revised in 1962 to select immigrants on the basis of skills, ostensibly without discrimination of any kind. However, race-based restrictions continued to be applied to "Orientals" with respect to whom they could sponsor for immigration to Canada.[18] In government literature, the liberalizing of the immigration laws is attributed to a growing awareness of the injustice of racism, but it is important to note that at this time Canada was also faced with a shortage of skilled workers, a problem that could be fixed through such liberalizing. Problems resulting from a skills shortage in a changing economy were documented in the *Financial Post* in 1964:

> A skill squeeze has caught up with Canada. Jobs are available now but the men are not and shortages are reported through the skill scale from tradesmen to professionals. Good jobs are going begging, but the unemployed can't fill them.[19]

Businesses were having difficulties recruiting skilled workers. It was estimated that in the mid 1960s only 7 percent of the Canadian workforce had secondary schooling or better and that over 40 percent had not even finished primary school.

One of the features of Canadian immigration policy is its flexibility; processes have been defined in broad terms and extensive power of control has been centralized in the minister of immigration. Since the *Immigration Act* of 1869, there have been five formal immigration acts passed by parliament (1869, 1910, 1952, 1976 [enacted 1978], and 2001). Some of these acts involved radical changes of policy and practice while others merely tweaked existing legislation. As a result, most important immigration changes, such as the *Chinese Exclusion Act*, the *Continuous Passage Act* and the point system, have been made through orders-in-council. Many changes made through such administrative orders have over the years dramatically altered immigration policy and practices without allowing for any parliamentary or public debate. It was not until 1930 that the government was even required to publish orders-in-council. As a result there is not a robust tradition in Canada of debating immigration policy, even though such policy is an important factor in both our national identity and our international reputation. While the governments of the day have had extensive powers in shaping immigration policy, it must be remembered that even the most exclusionary policies, such as the *Chinese Exclusion Act*, were supported by public opinion.

The Door Opens, 1967 to the Present

The final overt race-based restrictions were removed in 1967 with the introduction of the point system to recruit skilled workers. Canada was the first country in the world to implement a point-based system for immigrant selection. Initially, points were allocated in nine categories: education, occupation, professional skill, age, arranged employment, personal characteristics, English and French language facility, existing relatives in Canada and intended settlement location within Canada, with a score of 50 out of 100 required to be considered for immigration. The point system is still in use today for the selection of skilled workers, but its configuration and criteria have been changed several times since 1967.

While the point system was used exclusively for the selection of workers destined for the labour market (now referred to as "economic immigrants"), from 1967 until 1995, the majority of immigrants to Canada, close to 60 percent, entered as Family Class, consisting of sponsored relatives of Canadian citizens (more detail in Chapter 3). In 1983, for example, Family Class made up 55 percent of all immigrants to Canada and Economic Class was 27 percent. In 1995, immigration policies were re-engineered to prioritize economic immigrants, reversing the long-established pattern, and since 1996, economic immigrants have comprised close to 60 percent of the total.

Although the point system removed selection criteria based on race, there was not an immediate shift in the profile of immigrants to

Canada. Despite an increased diversity of immigrants from around the world, the dominance of Britain and the United States as the main source countries to Canada was unchanged until 1978 (see Table 1.1). In reality, this dominance lasted until 1982 as it was only the influx of Vietnamese refugees in 1979 and 1980 that displaced Britain and the United States as the top two source countries. From 1987 onwards, however, neither Britain nor the United States have been the top source countries to Canada. From 1987 to 1997, Hong Kong was the number one source country and from 1998 to 2009 China was in the top spot. Since 1995, India has been the number two source country to Canada (see Appendix 1 for a complete list). All of the top source countries since 1989, with the exception of Poland, were countries that were formerly banned from entry into Canada only fifty-two years earlier. The large influx of Polish migration was part of a massive exodus from 1981 to 1989 in which people were fleeing political oppression. In total, 95,202 Poles arrived in Canada, mostly as Convention refugees (discussed in Chapter 2).

Table 1.1 Summary of Top Source Countries to Canada

Time Period	Top Two Source Countries
1968–1982	Britain, United States
1983	U.S., India
1984–1985	Vietnam, Hong Kong
1986	U.S., India
1987–1988	Hong Kong, India
1989–1991	Hong Kong, Poland
1992	Hong Kong, Philipines
1993	Hong Kong, India
1994	Hong Kong, Philipines
1995–1997	Hong Kong, India
1998–2008	China, India

THE EVOLUTION OF IMMIGRATION POLICY 31

As time has passed, and especially since the 1980s, immigrants have increasingly belonged to racialized communities. Table 1.1 shows how the Canadian government has accepted immigrants from different source countries. Immigration has contributed to increasing the diversity of the Canadian population to such an extent that in the 2006 Canadian Census, there were more than two hundred different ethnic origins reported by respondents. Further, 75 percent of all immigrants who arrived between 2001 and 2006 were from racialized communities.[20] Most immigrants are from former "non-traditional" source countries in South and Southeast Asia. Residents born outside of Canada comprise 19.8 percent of the Canadian population, one of the highest rates in the world. In large urban centres, however, the percentage is much higher; in Toronto, for example, half of the population was born outside of Canada.

The point system criteria have shifted over time, with some criteria becoming more heavily weighted and others being dropped off the assessment altogether (see Table 1.2). Language facility, education and work experience have all become increasingly important in the selection of immigrants. Work experience, for example, is currently the third highest weighted requirement; it would be difficult for an individual to receive a passing mark as a skilled worker without receiving the maximum 21 points for four years of relevant work experience. In contrast, from 1967 to 1992, there were no points allocated for work experience. In 1992, work experience was added as a selection criterion, worth 8 out of a possible 112 points (7 percent). In 2002, the point system was again revised, with work experience elevated to one of the most important criteria (see Appendix 2 for detailed breakdown of the current criteria). Although this ensures that all Skilled Workers arrive in Canada with relevant international work experience, immigrant professionals report that their experience is almost entirely devalued by Canadian employers (discussed further in Chapter 3). Although points for occupation were dropped in 2003 and no longer a factor in the point calculation, the regulations allow application by only certain occupations, such as social workers, insurance adjusters and health-care workers (see Chapter 2 for complete list).

From the late 1960s until 1986, there was a direct link between the economic performance of Canada and the number of immigrants admitted. In periods of economic difficulty with high levels of unemployment (the early 1970s and the early 1980s), immigration numbers were significantly reduced. In 1983, in the midst of an economic recession, for example, there were only 89,157 immigrants admitted to Canada. In 1986, despite the economic outlook, the federal government decided to take a long-term approach to immigration, regardless of the immediate economic situation. Immigration targets were increased, and in 1989, the government set out a five-year plan with a goal of re-

Table 1.2 Point System Criteria, 1967, 1992 and 2007

Criteria	Points 1967	Points 1992	Points 2003
Education	20	16	25
Language ability	10	15	24
Work experience		8	21
Age	10	10	10
Adaptability			10
Arranged employment	10	10	10
Occupation	15	10	
Education training factor	20	18	
Demographic factor		10	
Close relative in Canada		5	
Personality	15	10	
Settlement area	5		
Total points	105	112	100
Passing mark	50	70	67

cruiting 250,000 immigrants each year, roughly 1 percent of the population.

The introduction of the point system marks a transition from selection criteria that give priority to race to ones that prioritize class. By replacing explicit race-based criteria in 1967 with a system that prioritizes education, profession and language proficiency, the government targets middle-class professionals of all races. Indeed, the result of this immigration selection process has been the creation of a large pool of highly educated immigrants from all over the world. At the highest levels of education, immigrants are much more educated than Canadian-born; almost 20 percent of all immigrants have a graduate degree, compared to just over 5 percent for Canadian-born. Further, while just over 16 percent of Canadian-born have a bachelor's degree, the rate is almost 32 percent for recent immigrants. The education rates are even higher for immigrants who have immigrated to Canada within the past five years.[21]

Conclusion

The history of immigration to Canada is not a story of fairness, equality and respect. Although Canada is now known for our open immigration policy and people from all over the world migrate to Canada, it was not always this way. It is important to be aware of the overt racism and sexism that guided the building of Canada in order to understand how current discrimination is connected to practices of the past. Although explicitly race-based restrictions were removed from immigration policy in 1967, research on labour market integration clearly demonstrates that racial discrimination has not been eliminated.[22] While current immigration policies are sharply focused on the potential economic impact of immigrants, it is important to keep in mind that immigrants impact their communities in more than economic ways; they also bring cultural and linguistic diversity and contribute to the social fabric of the community. In the next chapter we examine the current immigration policy in detail.

2. IMMIGRATION POLICY AND PRACTICES
The Mechanics of Migration

> Canada is looking for talented people, looking for the best and the brightest to come here.[1]

Canada enjoys a global reputation as a peaceful, fair and progressive country with institutionalized human rights protection. Not only is Canada a signatory to the most progressive global human rights documents such as the United Nations *Universal Declaration of Human Rights* (1948) and the United Nations *Convention Relating to the Status of Refugees* (1951), but we have also developed our own human rights legislation such as the Canadian *Bill of Rights* (1960), the Canadian *Human Rights Act* (1977) and the *Charter of Rights and Freedoms* (1982). These international and national human rights documents were the result of struggles of people who were subjected to unfair laws and practices. In Canada, historically, Chinese, Japanese, Ukrainian, South Asians, Jewish, First Nations, Métis, Inuit and others were subjected to discriminatory laws and practices based on their race and/or ethnicity. The formalization of human rights into policy has been a major step forward in Canada, but to what extent do the policies get put into practice? The following two incidents reveal that acts of discrimination based on notions of race and ethnicity continue in the present day:

On September 26, 2002, Maher Arar, a Canadian citizen, was taken into custody at Kennedy Airport in the United States where he was on a routine flight stopover, enroute to Montreal. He was detained for twelve days and questioned about links to Al-Qaeda. Although Arar repeatedly stated that he had no links to any terrorist organization, at the end of the questioning instead of being allowed to continue home to Toronto, he was put on a flight to Syria, his country of birth. He was transferred to a Syrian prison where the interrogation intensified. Although he strongly denied any connections, he was tortured, and detained for almost thirteen months. During his detention his partner, Monia Mazigh, went public with her husband's case, and alongside Amnesty International, appealed to the government for his release. When Arar returned to Canada he made a statement detailing the events of his detention and torture. The Canadian government ordered a commission of inquiry, which established that Arar had no links to terrorism and that he had been tortured. In January 2007, Mr. Arar was awarded $10 million in damages by the federal government.

Lake Simcoe is a popular fishing destination in Ontario about ninety minutes northeast of Toronto. For Asian Canadian anglers, this enjoyable activity was marred by a practice called "nipper tipping" by local residents. In 2006 and 2007, several Asian Canadian anglers reported being assaulted, thrown in the water and having their tackle destroyed by assailants. In 2007, one local man was charged with six counts of aggravated assault and two counts of criminal negligence when he physically assaulted a group of seven anglers, five Asian and two white Canadian men. When they tried to escape in their car, he proceeded to chase them, ramming their car with his pickup truck. The car was forced off the road into a tree; one of the men sustained serious permanent brain damage. The Ontario Supreme Court investigated these crimes and ruled that it was a hate crime. Although the Crown had requested a sentence of eight to ten years, the accused was given a punishment of two years less a day. When the sentencing was announced, one Asian-Canadian man in the courtroom shouted, "There is no justice in Canada." After the sentencing, Avvy Go, the director of the Metro Toronto Chinese and Southeast Asian Legal Clinic, read a statement on behalf of several Asian-Canadian groups, that included the following text: "This crime makes us feel we are unwanted in Canada, and it angers us to think that, in this day and age, we must still justify our identity as Canadians. Even at the best of times, many of us — especially those who live in smaller communities — often feel alienated and marginalized as we frequently encounter racist taunts which causes us to question our sense of belonging. Despite that fact, most of us do not dwell on the issue of racism in our daily lives. This crime cruelly reminds us that racial hatred is alive and well in Canada, and that as Asian-Canadians we are still vulnerable in this society; that we still cannot expect to enjoy equal rights and freedoms as others under the law because of our race. This crime is an extreme manifestation of the all too common sentiment that Asians are not "real" Canadians. We are made to feel like we are intruders and outsiders who can be assaulted at random simply because of what we are, and not what we do."

While these current examples of overt discrimination against immigrants and people of colour may seem to be detached and isolated, they are in fact deeply connected to historical immigration policy and practices that sought to establish and preserve Canada as a white country.

This chapter outlines the current immigration policy, the various categories of immigration and how they work. Because immigration is a topic that many Canadians have strong views about, it is important to be familiar with how the system works in order to understand how to interpret comments about immigration in newspaper articles, government reports and online forums. The chapter concludes with a critique of the current immigration system. As you read about how the immigration system is organized, pay attention to what requirements are needed for each of the categories and how the categories are named. What people are eligible to immigrate to Canada? What are the rules? Under what conditions can people enter Canada as permanent residents? What is the impact of the point system on the composition of immigrants in Canada? Would you and your family members be able to score enough points to qualify for immigration as Skilled Workers?

The Current System

There is no doubt that immigration is complex, involving the federal and provincial governments, employers, post-secondary institutions, communities, Canadians citizens, immigrants and refugees. Under the 2001 *Immigrant and Refugee Protection Act*, the current legislation, there are seven sub-sections of permanent residents grouped into three categories:

- Economic (Skilled Workers; Québec-selected Skilled Workers; Canadian Experience Class; Investors, Entrepreneurs and Self-Employed people; Provincial Nominees);
- Family Class; and
- Humanitarian (refugees).

Alongside the permanent resident categories, there is also a growing and controversial Temporary Worker recruitment program for occupations ranging from service sector and agricultural work to professional services (see Chapter 5). As detailed in Section 95 of the *Constitution Act 1867*, the federal government and the provinces both have power in the immigration process. As long as the provinces do not pass laws that are "repugnant to any Act of the Parliament

Table 2.1 Permanent Residents by Category in 2008

Immigrant Category	Admitted	
	Number	Percent
Skilled Workers	103,736	42.0
Business immigrants	12,407	5.0
Provincial/Territorial nominees	22,418	9.1
Live-In Caregivers*	10,511	4.3
Total Economic Class (including dependants)	149,072	60.3
Spouses, partners, children and others	48,970	19.8
Parents and grandparents	16,597	6.7
Total Family Class	65,567	26.5
Government-assisted refugees	7,295	3.0
Privately sponsored refugees	3,512	1.4
Protected persons in Canada	6,994	2.8
Dependants abroad	4,059	1.6
Total protected persons	21,860	8.8
Humanitarian and compassionate grounds/public policy	10,627	4.3
Permit holders	115	0
Total others	10,742	4.3
Category not stated	2	0
Total number of immigrants admitted as permanent residents	247,243	100
Total number of temporary workers	271,909	

* This category includes live-in caregivers who change status to permanent residents
Source: Citizenship and Immigration Canada, "A Commitment to Foreign Credential Recognition: Government of Canada Progress Report 2009," at <http://www.credentials.gc.ca/about/pdf/progress-report2009.pdf> (2009).

of Canada," they can participate in setting the selection criteria for immigrants and procedures for immigration.

While historically the government of Québec has played an active role in the selection of immigrants since 1971, the federal government has been the main player in immigration policy. However, the provinces have begun to take a more substantial role in the process through the Provincial Nominees Program. These federal-provincial agreements pertain exclusively to the selection of economic migrants; the federal government remains solely responsible for defining categories of immigration, setting immigration levels and establishing eligibility requirements. Recently, post-secondary institutions and employers have become increasingly active in immigrant selection through the Canadian Experience Class, Live-In Caregiver and Temporary Worker programs.

Each year, the federal government sets targets for total immigration, broken down by category. The goal of the government has been to recruit the equivalent of 1 percent of the Canadian population each year to keep the population growing and to meet labour market needs. In 2008, Economic Class immigrants represented 60 per cent of the total, with Family Class making up 26.5 percent and protected persons 8.8 percent (see Table 2.1). Each year a similar number of women and men immigrate to Canada. In 2008, the number of women was 128,629 and the number of men was 118,614. A gender analysis of the immigration categories, however, reveals that in the Skilled Worker and Business classifications women are more likely to be considered dependants rather than principal applicants. Although women made up 47.6 percent of the total Skilled Workers for 2008, only 34.2 percent of them were principal applicants; 57.3 percent were spouses or dependants.

Economic Class
Skilled Workers
Skilled Workers are selected on the basis of their potential to contribute to the economy. Currently, to qualify as a Skilled Worker, the largest subsection of the Economic Class, an applicant must score at least 67 out of 100 points in the point system. Points are awarded for education, work experience, age, English and

French language facility, arranged employment in Canada and the educational qualifications of the principal applicant's spouse (see Appendix 2 for a complete breakdown of the point allocation). From February 28, 2008, to June 26, 2010, in addition to these criteria, an applicant either had to have arranged employment or education and work experience in one of thirty-eight "priority occupations" to be considered. These occupations, roughly categorized into eight groupings, were identified through a series of government consultations and reflect the labour market needs, as defined by the federal government in 2007. This list of priority occupations was revised on June 26, 2010, to reduce the set of priority occupations to twenty-nine. The changes also introduced an annual limit of 20,000 Skilled Worker applications and mandatory third-party language assessments.

The idea of restricting Skilled Worker immigration to specific occupations is not new, having been implemented twice in the past thirty years. Critics of this approach raise questions about how well this list can reflect changing labour market needs. In the period between February 2008 and July 2010, there was an economic recession, a state bailout of the corporate sector and a reconfiguration of the labour market away from manufacturing to services. Yet, the priority occupations remained the unchanged throughout this period. In 2008, when this list was introduced, many provinces expressed concerns about the ability of the priority occupations to meet their specific labour market requirements. The sharp increase in the use of the Provincial Nominee Program is clearly one way that the provinces are working around this rigid federal system. For example, in 2005, there were 8,047 Provincial Nominee principal applicants, spouses and dependents; in 2009 this number had risen by over 350 percent, to 30,369. The new annual maximum of 20,000 Skilled Worker applications is certain to cause a further increase in the use of Provincial Nominee Program.

Either explicitly or implicitly, the assessment of Skilled Workers has always been linked to labour market needs; however, prior to the

2008 restriction, all applications were considered for immigration. Not only did these changes restrict the eligibility for Skilled Worker applicants, it removed the obligation for the government to process all applications. According to the government, these changes were made in order to deal with a backlog of over 640,000 Skilled Worker applications, which were taking up to six years to process. More than two years after these changes, the backlog is still huge, standing at 380,000 applications.

Immigrating to Canada is neither a quick nor an inexpensive process. The fees vary according to how many people are involved in the application. The current costs are $550 for a single person and $1,400 for a two-parent family with two children. Each person who is immigrating must take, pass and pay for a medical examination, a criminal record check and a language proficiency test. If any of the applicants is found to be either a danger to public health or safety or a potential drain on health or social services, the application is denied. The applicant is also required to show "proof of funds" to

The Twenty-nine Priority Occupations (effective June 26, 2010)

- managers (primary production [except agriculture], business services)
- insurance adjusters and claims examiners
- biologists and related scientists
- architects
- social workers
- psychologists
- health care (specialist, general and family physicians, dentists, pharmacists, physiotherapists, registered nurses, medical radiation technologists, dental hygienists & dental therapist, licensed practical nurses)
- food production (managers, chefs and cooks)
- contractors and supervisors in the trades (carpentry, mechanic trades, electricians, plumbers, welders, heavy-duty equipment mechanics, crane operators, drillers and blasters — surface mining, quarrying and construction, oil and gas drilling and service).

the immigration officer at the time of application. These funds are to ensure that the applicant and their family will be financially self-sufficient when they arrive in Canada. The amount depends on the number of people included in the application. For a single applicant, the amount is $10,833, and for a two-parent family with two children, the amount is $20,130. This "proof of funds" requirement is waived if the principal applicant has arranged employment in Canada.

Québec-Selected Skilled Workers

Since 1971, there has been a formal immigration arrangement between the Canadian government and the government of Québec. The most recent, signed on April 1, 1991, outlines Québec's role in determining levels of immigration to the province. While Québec has the authority and responsibility to set annual targets as well as to establish its own selection criteria for Skilled Workers, the federal government continues to have authority over the selection of Family and Humanitarian Class immigrants. Skilled Workers applying to immigrate to Québec are evaluated by a set of selection factors, different from the point system, that includes: an applicant's profile, training, work experience, knowledge of French and English, ties to Québec, arranged employment in Québec and information regarding an accompanying spouse or common-law partner. Procedurally, an immigrant applies to the Québec government for a Certificat de sélection du Québec. If successful, the applicant then applies to Citizenship and Immigration Canada for permanent residence. In addition to passing the standard medical examination and security checks, the applicant must demonstrate that they have enough money to support themselves for the first three months after immigration. The amounts specified for 2009 range from $2,748 for a single person to $4,872 for two parents with two children.

The Québec assessment is unique in that it includes information about the regulation of professions, giving immigrants clear information about what they need to do in order to receive a licence, if it is necessary for their profession. As we discuss in Chapter 3, up-to-date information is critical for immigrant professionals who are seeking to establish a practice in Canada.

Business Immigration

The Business Immigration Program, first introduced in 1976, aims to recruit experienced investors, entrepreneurs and self-employed persons to Canada. For all three business sub-classes a modified point system is used. The selection criteria include five elements: business experience (35 points), education (25 points), age (10 points), language abilities (24 points) and adaptability (6 points). The education, age and language abilities criteria are identical to the federal Skilled Workers points allocation. For the most heavily weighted category, business experience, 20 points are given for two years' experience, 25 for three, 30 for four and 35 for five and above. The 6 points for adaptability can be gained if the applicant has made a trip to Canada that is deemed by the province of destination as a business exploration trip within five years of the application date. A score of 35 points out of 100 is considered to be a pass.

In 2008, Business immigrants formed 5 percent of the total immigrants to Canada. Even though this is a small percentage, these programs have been criticized internationally as allowing rich people to buy their way into Canada[2]; there is no doubt that for the Canadian government, the Investor and Entrepreneur programs provide a valuable source of capital.

Investors

Investors are established business people who are expected to make a significant investment in the Canadian economy. In their application for immigration, they must demonstrate that they have at least two years' business experience and a minimum net worth of $1.6 million dollars. They must make an investment of $800,000 in Canada, a lump-sum payment which is managed and invested by Citizenship and Immigration Canada (CIC). The investment is held for a period of five years by CIC, after which time it is returned to the investor without interest. Like other classes of immigrants, investors have to demonstrate that they have enough money to support themselves, as well as passing medical and security checks. The funds generated from this program, as of June 2010, were close to $2 billion dollars.

Entrepreneurs
The Entrepreneur Program targets experienced business people who plan on managing their own businesses in Canada. To qualify they must demonstrate that they have two years of international business experience, including managing a qualifying business and having a percentage of equity in the business within a specific time period. They also need to demonstrate that they have a minimum net worth of $300,000, that they meet the selection criteria for the Entrepreneur Program as well as passing the medical and security screening. In order to become a permanent resident, an Entrepreneur landed immigrant must own a one-third share of a Canadian business that they also manage, as well as create new full-time positions in the business.

Self-Employed Persons
The Self-Employed Persons Program is aimed at immigrants who intend on being self-employed in a cultural, athletic or agricultural industry in Canada. The selection process takes into account relevant experience, a point system identical to the Entrepreneur Program (except that Business Experience is replaced by a category called "Relevant Experience"), medical and security checks, and a proof of funds requirement that is identical to the Skilled Worker program. Relevant experience includes participation at a world-class level in cultural activities or athletics, or experience in farm management leading to purchasing and managing a farm in Canada.

Live-In Caregivers
The Live-In Caregiver Program covers workers who provide care for children, elderly people or persons with disabilities in private homes. The workers must live in the home where they are employed. The qualifications of the applicant include the successful completion of the equivalent of Canadian secondary school, defined as twelve years of schooling, good working knowledge of English or French, and at least six months' training or a minimum of one year of recent full-time relevant international work experience. The applicant also needs to provide three documents: a job confirmation letter from a Canadian employer approved by Human Resources and Social Development Canada; a written contract from the prospective employer outlining hours of work, salary, duties and benefits approved by Citizenship and Immigration Canada; and a valid Canadian work permit. Québec applicants need to first obtain a Certificate of Acceptance from the Québec government.

This two-stage program first admits Live-In Caregivers as temporary workers, and providing they are able to work and pay taxes for two years (or 3,900 hours) of their four-year contract, they are eligible to apply for permanent residency at the end of their contract. After they become permanent residents they can sponsor family members that are living abroad for Canadian citizenship. In 2008, of 6,157 Live-In Caregiver principal applicants, 5,826 (95 percent) were women.

Provincial Nominees

With the exception of the North West Territories and Nunavut, all provincial and territorial governments have agreements with the federal government to address specific labour market shortages through nominating immigrants for permanent settlement. For these arrangements, a prospective applicant first applies to the province, and similar to the Québec-selected Skilled Worker Program, they then apply to the federal government with their successful assessment. To be accepted by the province, the applicant must have secured employment.

Each province has its own programs, selection and assessment tools, and qualifying levels. Since the provincial nominees are not assessed on the federal point system, they are able to shop around, to see where their skills might be in demand. For example, electrical engineering is not on the federal "priority occupation" list, yet it is on the "skills shortage list" for the Yukon Territory. As a result, an electrical engineer applying to the federal Skilled Worker Program would have their application rejected outright. By first applying to the Yukon Territory as a Provincial Nominee, an applicant can bypass federal selection criteria and, according to the Yukon government website, will have their application processed in six weeks. After the province has issued a Certificate of Acceptance, the federal government processes the application, including the requirement for a medical examination, security and criminal checks, and the proof of funds. It has been argued that this system of provincial nominations increasingly positions provinces against each other as competitors for Skilled Workers.

Canadian Experience Class

On September 17, 2008, the federal government introduced the Canadian Experience Class (CEC), a new immigration category created to facilitate the transition from temporary to permanent status for international students and high-skill temporary workers. To be eligible for this program, international students who have graduated from a Canadian post-secondary institution require a minimum of one year of full-time skilled work experience; for temporary workers, the requirement is two years. For both groups of applicants, skilled work includes managerial, professional and technical occupations as well as skilled trades (Canadian National Occupational Classification (NOC) levels 0, A and B).[3] Temporary workers who perform work considered semi-skilled or low-skilled in agriculture, the resource industries or manufacturing are not eligible for this program. The application for the CEC program can be made from abroad or from within Canada and is subject to the following fees: $550 for the principal applicant, $550 for a spouse and $150 per child. In addition, the applicant has to successfully pass a language assessment test.

The initial goal of the federal government for 2008 was to admit between 10,000 and 12,000 immigrants in this class. Due to the later-than-expected start of the program, the federal government anticipated taking in between 5,000 and 7,500 immigrants through the CEC Program in 2009, and initial projections for 2010 were a great deal higher. Interestingly, revised 2010 projections indicate only between 2,670 to 2,856 CEC entrants. While there were only 2,544 CEC immigrants in 2009, the potential for this category is great. The Canadian Chamber of Commerce (2008), a supporter of the CEC Program, anticipates that this new immigration category could add up to 30,000 skilled immigrants annually. This figure seems quite conservative when you consider Citizenship and Immigration Canada's estimation that there were 196,227 international students in Canada on December 1, 2009.

Family Class

It is the right of every Canadian citizen or permanent resident of Canada who is over the age of eighteen to sponsor specific family members for Canadian citizenship. There are two different processes for sponsoring family members, depending on the closeness of the relationship.

Spouses, Partners and Dependent Children

The first grouping of relatives includes spouses, partners and dependent children. A spouse is a person of the same or opposite sex who is legally married to the sponsor. A common-law partner is a person of the same or opposite sex who has been living with the sponsor for a continuous twelve-month period. A conjugal partner is common-law partner who has not been able to meet the twelve-month living together criterion due to immigration barriers, discrimination based on sexual orientation or lack of access to divorce. A dependent child is under the age of twenty-two and without a spouse or partner, or is financially dependent on the parent due to being a full-time student or having a disability.

Both the applicant and the sponsor must meet certain conditions. First, the applicant must be over sixteen years of age and must pass medical, criminal and background screening, which may involve obtaining a certificate from the police authorities in their home country. Those who are deemed to pose a risk to Canada's security, such as those with a criminal record, are not allowed to enter Canada.[4]

The sponsor also has a list of stringent criteria, including agreeing to provide financial support to the applicant for a certain period of time (three years for a spouse or partner, ten years for a child or until the child turns twenty-five, whichever comes first). A formal sponsorship agreement outlines the financial support conditions, stating that although the sponsor is responsible for the applicant's support and ensures that the applicant will not draw on government assistance during the specified time period, the applicant will attempt to provide for their own expenses. In addition to the income requirement, the sponsor has be eighteen years of age or older, and if they live in Québec, they have to meet Québec's immigration sponsorship requirements. While it is necessary for the sponsor to be a Canadian citizen or landed immigrant, there is no requirement that they are living in Canada at the time of the application. A person is not allowed to sponsor a relative if they:

- failed to provide financial support agreed to when a sponsorship agreement to sponsor another relative was signed in the past;
- defaulted on a court-ordered support order, such as alimony or child support;
- received government financial assistance for reasons other than a disability;
- were convicted of a violent criminal offence, any offence against a relative or any sexual offence — depending on circumstances such as the nature of the offence, how long ago it occurred and

whether a pardon was issued;
- defaulted on an immigration loan — late or missed payments;
- are in prison; or
- have declared bankruptcy and have not been released from it yet.

The government also states that there are other factors which would make an applicant ineligible to sponsor a relative, but these factors are not listed.

The application is processed both at offices in Canada and abroad, and while the processing time is constantly changing, at the time of writing, an application for family reunification takes eleven weeks to process at the Mississauga office. There is also an assessment of the application in an international Canadian visa office, at which 80 percent of the applications are, on average, processed within twelve months. The time, however, varies substantially depending on the geographic location. For example, in Nairobi, 80 percent of the applications are processed in twenty-six months; in Beijing it is five months. It is important to remember that 20 percent of applications take longer than this to process and some cases take a very long time to complete. Currently, an application to sponsor a spouse or partner would cost $1,590 plus $150 for every dependent child.

Eligible Relatives

This second grouping of Family Class includes parents and grandparents and other relations under certain conditions. A citizen can also sponsor brothers, sisters, nephews, nieces and grandchildren who are orphaned, under eighteen years of age and not married or in a common-law relationship. Further, if the sponsor has no family in Canada and they do not have any relatives in the previous list to sponsor, they are eligible to sponsor another relative of any age or relationship. Siblings over the age of eighteen and adult independent children are, however, excluded from this category.

The eligibility criteria for the applicant and the sponsor are identical for the process to sponsor spouses, partners and dependent children. The sponsorship assessment process, though similar, has a few differences. One difference is that in order to sponsor relatives in this grouping, the sponsor must be living in Canada. A second significant difference relates to the length of time the sponsor agrees to be responsible for the financial support of the applicant. For eligible relatives the sponsor must agree to provide financial support to the applicant for three to ten years, depending on the applicant's age and relationship to the sponsor. Unlike the process for spouses, partners and dependent children, this time period does not begin until the applicant becomes a permanent resident.

Compared to the processing time for spousal and partner applications, the process to bring other eligible relatives to Canada is significantly slower. Currently, for sponsorship applications for parents and grandparents, applications are spending three years in the queue before they are even started. The processing time is also longer for the in-Canada assessment, currently taking thirty-six months to complete. The same guidelines for processing times at international visa offices are in place. So, if a Canadian citizen wanted to sponsor their parent from Nairobi, the minimum processing time would be ninety-seven months, or just over eight years. The application fee, paid at the time the application is submitted, is $1740.

Refugees

In 1951, the Office of the United Nations High Commissioner for Refugees held a conference to discuss the status of refugees.[5] The *Convention Relating to the Status of Refugees* was signed by twenty-six countries in Geneva (this is why it is commonly referred to as the Geneva Convention). It developed a working definition of a refugee and outlines the rights and responsibilities of nations that grant asylum to refugees. Developed in the context of the massive displacement of Europeans after World War II, the initial definition included specific references to Europe and particular time periods. In the revised 1967 Protocol, these restrictive time and geographic conditions were removed, making the definition more inclusive. This 1967 definition of a refugee is still used today and describes a refugee as a person who,

> owing to a well-founded fear of being persecuted for reasons of race, religion, nationality, membership of a particular social group, or political opinion, is outside the country of their nationality, and is unable to or, owing to such fear, is unwilling to avail themselves of the protection of that country.

Although Canada was involved in the 1951 Convention and helped develop the document, the Canadian government did not officially sign the Convention until 1969. According to the Canadian Council for Refugees,[6] the delay in signing the agreement was in part due to fears of the RCMP that the new guidelines would restrict Canada's ability to deport refugees for security reasons.

It was not until 1978 that refugees were formally included in immigration policy. Prior to this, there was no overarching policy to guide the decision-making process for people in need of protection and relocation. Despite the lack of formal policy, Canada did admit groups of refugees prior to 1978 from areas experiencing revolutions and massive political upheaval (over 37,000 Hungarians in 1956, 11,000 Czechs in 1968, more than 7,000 Asians from Uganda in 1973 and close to 1,200 Chileans in 1975). Over time the definition of refugee has evolved. In Canada, for example, women, gay men and lesbians have been recognized as "members of a particular social group" and have been able to secure rights as refugees. A refugee is different from an immigrant, in that an immigrant is a person who plans to leave their home country to settle permanently in another country. Refugees are forced to flee sometimes without warning, under traumatic circumstances such as persecution, war, political oppression and natural disaster.

Canada has two refugee programs, the Refugee and Humanitarian Resettlement Program (for people applying from outside of Canada) and the In-Canada Asylum Program. Most refugees in the Refugee and Humanitarian Resettlement Program are recruited from refugee camps. Both the government and private sponsors are able to bring refugees to Canada. While refugees are granted permanent residence upon arrival, they are responsible for the costs of the medical examinations and transportation. As a result, many refugees start their life in Canada with a financial burden. Another issue facing refugees and their sponsors is the processing time for applications, which can be so long that private sponsors lose hope.

The goal of the In-Canada Asylum Program is to provide protection to people in Canada at risk of torture or cruel or unusual punishment in their home country. In 2007, according to Citizenship and Immigration Canada, 28,000 people claimed asylum status upon arriving in Canada. But after arriving, many people are denied entry for various reasons, such as having a criminal record, having had previous refugee claims denied or arriving from a country that is considered to be a "safe third country." A safe third country is a county that is judged on the basis of its human rights record and stated commitment to international human rights conventions to be a safe location for refugees to make claims for asylum. In 2004, the Safe Third Country Agreement was ratified by Canada and the United States, creating a requirement for refugees to make a claim in the country in which they arrive. This means that refugees who arrive in the United States cannot make a refugee claim in Canada as the United States is considered a safe haven. There is a great deal of debate around how a safe third country can be assessed, and whether or not this agreement is serving as a gatekeeper for refugees to Canada. The Canadian Council for Refugees has argued that the United States is not safe for all refugees due to its history of detaining refugees for extended periods of time and for failing to protect refugee rights. The In-Canada Asylum Program has also been criticized for slow processing times of applications, with reported times of up to eight years to finalize claims with negative decisions.[7]

Critiques of Immigration Policy

If you find the current immigration policy confusing, you are probably not alone. First, while we talk about the point system as a singular entity, we do not employ a single system of assessment. Between the seven economic classes of immigration, there are thirteen different configurations of the point system, with separate evaluation criteria for federal Skilled Workers, Québec Skilled Workers, Business Class immigrants and for each province that participates in the Provincial Nominee Program. The other immigration classes, Live-In Caregivers, Canadian Experience Class, Family Class and Humanitarian, all use assessment criteria for selection, but they do not use a point system. The diversity of immigration categories, assessment criteria and differing levels of jurisdiction makes for a complex system.

While the federal government is constitutionally mandated to administer immigration, its role in immigration is becoming noticeable weaker. With the dramatic rise of Provincial Nominees, Temporary Workers, Canadian Experience Class and Live-In Caregivers, and the simultaneous limiting of Skilled Worker applications to 20,000 annually, employers, post-secondary educational institutions and provincial governments are increasingly becoming key players in immigrant selection. Employers directly select both Temporary Workers and Live-In Caregivers, and are central to the Provincial Nominee Program, as arranged employment is a requirement. Post-secondary educational institutions set selection criteria for international students, who then become potential applicants for the Canadian Experience Class. The provinces are increasingly selecting their own Skilled Workers through the Provincial Nominee Program.

An analysis of the immigration trends over the past five years of reported data (see Table 2.2) shows that while the overall number of permanent residents has decreased slightly, there has been a dramatic increase in two categories. The Provincial Nominee Program

Table 2.2 Permanent Residents and Temporary Workers, 2005–2009

Category	2005	2006	2007	2008	2009
Skilled Workers — principal applicants	52,269	44,161	41,251	43,360	40,729
Skilled Workers — spouses and dependants	77,969	61,783	56,601	60,374	55,205
Total Skilled Workers	130,238	105,944	97,852	103,734	95,934
Entrepreneurs — principal applicants	750	820	581	446	372
Entrepreneurs — spouses and dependants	2,098	2,273	1,579	1,255	943
Total Entrepreneurs	2,848	3,093	2,160	1,701	1,315
Self-employed — principal applicants	302	320	203	164	179
Self-employed — spouses and dependants	714	632	373	341	358
Total Self Employed	1,016	952	576	505	537
Investors — principal applicants	2,591	2,201	2,025	2,832	2,872
Investors — spouses and dependants	7,020	5,830	5,420	7,370	7,437
Total Investors	9,611	8,031	7,445	10,202	10,309
Canadian Experience Class — principal applicants	-	-	-	-	1,774
Canadian Experience Class — spouses and dependants	-	-	-	-	770
Total Canadian Experience Class					2,544

Provincial Nominees — principal applicant	2,643	4,672	6,329	8,343	11,799
Provincial Nominees — spouses and dependants	5,404	8,664	10,765	14,075	18,570
Total Provincial Nominees	8,047	13,336	17,094	22,418	30,369
Live-In Caregivers — principal applicants	3,063	3,547	3,433	6,157	6,272
Live-In Caregivers — spouses and dependants	1,489	3,348	2,684	4,354	6,178
Total Live-In Caregivers	4,552	6,895	6,117	10,511	12,450
Total Economic Class	156,312	138,251	131,244	149,071	150,914
Total Family Class	63,361	70,512	66,238	65,574	65,187
Total Refugees	35,776	32,499	27,955	21,860	22,844
Total Permanent Residents	262,241	251,642	236,754	247,246	252,124
Temporary Workers (present on Dec. 1, 2009)	140,976	161,132	199,580	250,492	282,771

Source: Citizenship and Immigration Canada, "Facts and Figures 2009 — Immigration Overview: Permanent and Temporary Residents," at <cic.gc.ca/english/resources/statistics/facts2009/index.asp> (2010).

has increased 377 percent in five years, from 8,047 principal applicants, spouses and dependents in 2005 to 30,369 in 2009. The Live-In Caregiver Program has increased 274 percent in the same time period. The other notable increase is in the Temporary Worker Program, which has seen a 200 percent increase since 2005. It will be interesting to see how robust the Canadian Experience Class becomes in the future.

Also important to note is that over the last five years, some immigration categories have been reduced, notably the federal Skilled

Workers, Entrepreneurs, Self-Employed and Refugees. In the discourse on refugees in particular, the government likes to invoke an image of Canada as a country with a proud tradition of compassion and fairness. While Canada was praised in the early 1980s by the United Nations High Commission on Refugees for its welcome of Vietnamese refugees, the reduction in the number of refugees over the past five years, at a time when wars are actively being fought and political repression is ongoing, raises questions about Canada's commitment to providing protection for refugees.

The experience of the Chaudhry family in Halifax highlights how precarious life can be for refugees in Canada. Roouf and Fakhira Chaudhry travelled to Canada in 2003 with their child Rukhna, claiming refugee status on arrival. In Pakistan the family of Fakhira had arranged a marriage for her to a man she did not wish to marry. In her opposition to this marriage she faced beatings from her father and death threats from her extended family. She married Roouf secretly in Pakistan and her family has vowed to kill them. Returning to Pakistan, therefore, would certainly be a great threat to their safety and well-being. Since they have settled in Halifax they have had two children, worked in various jobs and integrated into the community. In 2006 their refugee application was denied, and as of September 2010 they were still waiting for the results of an appeal based on humanitarian and compassionate grounds. Living under a deportation order for the past four years has placed the family under a great deal of financial and psychological stress. No One Is Illegal, a national grassroots advocacy group, has launched a campaign raising awareness of this issue and organizing a community response to the Chaudhry family's situation.[8]

Summary

As we detailed in Chapter 1, prior to 1967, the suitability of immigrants as potential citizens was determined in large part by their race. While current immigration selection practices and policies no longer use overtly discriminatory criteria, they continue to be highly selective, recruiting the "best and brightest" by relying almost exclusively on economic indicators for permanent migration. A review of the immigration categories and processes reveals that it is not quick, inexpensive or easy to immigrate to Canada. The process to immigrate varies widely depending on the immigration class — Economic, Family or Humanitarian — a person falls under, and it is definitely not straightforward navigating the system. Most migrants who qualify for permanent settlement have advanced education, years of relevant international work experience, existing family connections or a lot of money.

Revisions to immigration policy and practice, such as the reduced number of priority occupations and the expansion of the Temporary Worker Program, expose a two-tiered, short-term approach by the government. In many ways the federal government is running the country like a business that relies on a temporary agency for its staffing. It is critical that we become familiar with how the system works and begin to challenge the policy changes to immigration that are done without public debate but have important consequences for Canadian society. What will be the impact of expanding the Temporary Worker Program? If we really care about global human rights, why has the number of refugees been reduced dramatically over the past five years? Is the government doing enough to ensure that highly skilled migrants will be able to actually contribute to the economy in meaningful ways? These are important questions, and since the government continues to make dramatic changes to immigration policy without public debate, we need to open up these issues for discussion. The next chapter addresses employment issues for immigrants. Once immigrants and refugees arrive in Canada they are often confronted with labour market barriers that are difficult to overcome, and they end up working in jobs far below their abilities.

3. IMMIGRANTS AND THE LABOUR MARKET
Devaluation, Frustration and Downward Mobility

The Daily Bread Food Bank[1] of Toronto reported that 46 percent of the 952,883 people who relied on the food bank for basic survival in 2007–2008 were immigrants. Thirty-seven percent of the immigrants had a minimum of one post-secondary credential, compared to 16 percent of Canadian-born food bank users. To understand why immigrants are experiencing poverty such as this in Toronto, the destination for 35 percent of all immigrants to Canada, we need to examine their labour market participation. What kinds of jobs are they getting? Are their wages and job responsibilities comparable to their Canadian-born counterparts? Are they able to find work in their areas of expertise? If they are not able to get jobs in their fields, what barriers are in their way and why are they there?

This chapter examines the labour market performance of immigrants. Following a general discussion of the issues, it examines the numerous labour market barriers identified by academic researchers, government task forces, community advocacy groups and immigrants themselves. These barriers include lack of credential assessment and recognition, devaluation of international work experience, limited opportunities to gain appropriate Canadian work experience, discrimination, lack of professional networks, difficulties adapting to Canadian culture, lack of knowledge of

Canadian standards and practices, cumbersome and costly licensing processes and employers' lack of knowledge of international systems. This chapter focuses on the devaluation of international credentials, work experience and professional networks. Finally, we analyze the underperformance of immigrants in the workplace with respect to the impact on the Canadian economy, social fabric and ability to innovate.

We open this chapter with an extended speech from Ivy Zheng, a mechanical engineer from China who immigrated to Canada in 2001. The speech was presented to the Creating Our Collective Action Plan Conference, organized by the Canadian Technology Human Resources Board to address issues of Canada's global competitiveness in the technology sector. Ms. Zheng had come to the conference organizers' attention because she had been featured in the *Toronto Star*. Her shocking story of deskilling and frustration became known through a series of articles focusing on the settlement experiences of newcomers to Canada. Why was a successful mechanical engineer from China working selling cinnamon buns in a Toronto subway station? Her story is quoted at length because it illuminates the struggles that many immigrants to Canada face (see Box: Ivy Zheng's Story).

Immigrants like Ivy Zheng are the result of an immigration selection process that is heavily weighted for education and work experience. As noted in Chapter 1, since 1995, approximately 60 percent of the immigrants to Canada are Economic immigrants with post-secondary education and years of international work experience. In comparison to the Canadian-born population, immigrants have higher levels of education. According to the 2006 Canadian Census, 20 percent of the Canadian-born population had at least one post-secondary degree while the percentage was 32 percent for people born outside of Canada. For immigrants who arrived in Canada between 2001 and 2006, the number was significantly higher, at 51 percent. Yet despite the advanced education of immigrants, highly skilled newcomers experience great difficulty in finding appropriate

Ivy Zheng's Story

I used to work in China Academy of Launch Vehicle Technology as a mechanical engineer. I designed different components which are used on electric and hydraulic control systems of the rockets. One key component I designed is still being used on the LM-2F rocket, which launched an astronaut to the space in October 15, 2003, in China. That critical piece of technology first shot into space during a test flight of the LM-2F rocket in 1999. The following year, I was honoured in a national competition for my work on the component, which has the extremely high reliability.

In late 2001, I immigrated to Canada and landed in Toronto. After settled down, I went to LINC to improve my English language skills. I spent two month there. As soon as I got the certificate of LINC level five I left school and started job searching. I made some friends during my study in the LINC. By their recommendation, I went to a job-searching workshop. I learnt resume and cover letter writing skills, basic rule of making cold calls, learnt how to follow up and how to try to find unpublished job openings. Then I tried. Almost every day, I was in Human Resources Centre. Surfed the Internet, wrote cover letters, changed my resumes, send resumes by fax machine and made cold calls. After a month, I was shocked. I didn't receive any response from the jobs I applied. None. I thought maybe my resume is not good. Then, I joined another one-week workshop to improve my job searching skills. At the same time, I tried to make more cold calls. Everyone knows cold call is not easy. It is even harder for our immigrants whose first language is not English. Another very important factor is, we are new, and our network is limited. We have no way to know someone who works in the field, which we want to step in. So, it is very hard to get a chance to talk to a human resources person. Usually the phone number we found from the website or yellow pages is the telephone switchboard of the company. Once I said I am looking for the job, the receptionist would tell me that "the person who does hiring wouldn't receive phone calls. Just send your resume by fax or by email. We will contact you if you are qualified." But no one contact me. There was only once, I reached a human resource person by chance. The only question he asked me was "do you have Canadian experience?" I answered him honestly: "I am new immigrant looking for my first job in Canada. But I had nine years of experience in mechanical engineering field in China." He said, "Sorry, we need someone who has Canadian experience." I was confused. The Canadian government gives me the visa as an independent skilled immigrant that means the government approves my foreign credentials. But why no Canadian company approves my experience. If no companies would give me the first chance, how can I gain the Canadian experience?!

One job counsellor told me, "Don't give up. Keep trying. You will find a professional job one day." But I couldn't. I spent more than half a year already at that time. There was another serious problem I had to face; my money is going to run out. I had to think about find a temporary job first to pay my rent and expenses.

Since I am good at computer and software, I think I can easily find a job in office at least. I applied for the secretary. They said I don't have Canadian experience. My goal goes down to receptionist. Still they told me I don't have Canadian experience. Then, data entry. I took the test of keyboard speed. It is 60 wpm. "Not too bad," the agency says, "but there are lots of local candidates who have the same input speed as you. It is easy to find them a job instead of you." Then, my goal goes down to cashier. I think I am good at mathematics at least; it shouldn't be a problem to dealing with money. Then, what happened? I couldn't find even a cashier job in food court in the Mall! They ask me again for Canadian experience in related field! Of course I don't have experience in cashier field. This is not my goal. I apply for these jobs just for survive. I have no choice! One day, after the store manager said sorry to me, I talked to one of cashiers working in the same store. She is a student, local, 17 years old, part-time. She told me it is her first job. Do you think a 17-years-old student has Canadian experience in cashier field before she stated working in the food court? At that moment, I realized that Canadian Experience is a very beautiful excuse for saying "our citizens only." I was so disappointed. I have work experience in my own professional field, I also have other different skills, but I cannot persuade anyone to take me seriously here in Canada.

Finally, I found my first job in a Chinese restaurant. Thanks to the experience there, I was able to switch to different labour jobs. Since part-time work cannot cover my expense, I have to work full-time. Even though, two thirds of my income pays to the rent. After eight hours standing and hard working, I feel exhausted. I even don't want to cook for myself sometimes. But I never stop job searching. I spent almost all my spare time on job searching. I know it is my only hope. If I give up, I will suffer in labour forever.

It is a vicious circle. We want to find a professional job. Once we

> couldn't, and we don't have enough money to support ourselves, we have to do the labour job. But once we start labour job, our time and energy getting limited. We have less chance to get a professional job. This is my story.
>
> Source: Ivy Zheng, "Conference Address," 2004, at <web.archive.org/web/20040213013652/http://www.cthrb.ca/English/Documents/CTHRBMiniSymposiumIvyZhengRemarks.doc>.

employment. In fact, the vast majority of immigrant professionals experience "occupational skidding,"[2] that is, they work in jobs that are unrelated to their education and experience. New immigrants are more likely to work in low-status, low paying jobs. According to the Longitudinal Survey of Immigrants to Canada (LSIC), in 2002, only four out of ten immigrants who were employed at the time of the survey were working in the profession or occupation in which they were educated and experienced.[3] The deprofessionalization of immigrants is becoming worse. A 2010 Statistics Canada study based on 2006 Census data showed that 62 percent of Canadian-educated professionals were working in their fields, but only 24 percent, or less than one in four immigrant professionals, had the same employment outcome.[4]

It has been argued that the Canadian government succeeds in its goal in attracting the "best and the brightest" people but fails dismally at integrating these new Canadians into the labour market:

> Right now we're suffering from short-term vision, explains Mr. Nixon [president and chief executive officer of the Royal Bank]. "We welcome immigrants who are next in the pipeline. We rely on temporary workers to fill our short-term needs and we hope for the best. We put newcomers through a cumbersome application process—even though they have the skills we urgently need. We don't fast-track the best talent. We make it hard for businesses to hire foreign talent, forcing them to prove skill

shortages—even when those shortages are well documented. And finally, we don't have the right infrastructure to support immigrants when they get here. We deny them good jobs because they have no Canadian work experience.[5]

As immigration trends have shifted since 1967, reflecting more varied source countries and increased annual quotas, recent immigrants have experienced greater difficulties in establishing themselves than immigrants of the past. Recent immigrants from racialized communities experience high levels of unemployment and underemployment. Despite the fact that professionals are rewarded during the immigration process for their education and skills, they face numerous barriers in gaining professional recognition from professional regulatory bodies, employers and universities, and these barriers significantly impact their labour market participation.

Immigrants are a diverse group with respect to race, gender, skills and education, and their social location affects the conditions of their settlement in Canada. However, there is a pronounced gap between the income levels of Canadian-born and immigrant university graduates. Drawing on data from the 2006 Census, researchers at the Toronto Immigrant Employment Data Initiative (TIEDI) showed that in 2005, while Canadian-born women earned on average $44,278 and Canadian-born men earned $81,416, immigrant women only made $28,346 and immigrant men earned $44,908. When these figures are desegregated according to period of immigration, a pattern emerges demonstrating that income decreases dramatically for the most recently arrived immigrants. For example, women who immigrated between 2001 and 2006 earned $14,861 and for men the figure was $25,417.[6]

It has been argued that the devaluation of international credentials and experience is rooted in the nature of capitalism, in the desire for employers to maximize profit. Just as employers utilize Canadian credentials as screening and selection devices for hiring, the Canadian government is using educational criteria as an assessment tool for skilled immigrants. The goal of these policies is to increase Canada's competitiveness in the global marketplace, and they are based on the belief that higher levels of formal education will lead to greater economic success. It is important to note that while the education levels of immigrants continues to rise, so too have the education levels of Canadian-born. Whereas in the late 1960s, only 7 percent of Canadians had finished secondary school, in 2006, 20 percent have a university degree. Underemployment is a phenomenon that impacts both immigrants and Canadian-born, and for most jobs, workers' skills exceed the requirements.

Key Reports

Since the late 1980s, and especially since 1995, there has a vast body of literature written on the labour market integration of immigrants to Canada. The barriers faced by immigrants have been documented by public and private bodies including a royal commission, parliamentary committees, task forces, foundations, social policy think tanks, community-based agencies and academics. Many of these studies have been funded by the federal or provincial governments. In the early 1990s, there was a tendency for reports to focus on issues facing a particular ethno-cultural population across professions; in the late 1990s, there was a shift to focus on barriers for a particular profession across ethno-cultural lines.

One of the first reports to identify the barriers facing immigrants in Canada was *Equality in Employment: A Royal Commission Report* by Judge Rosalie Silberman Abella.[7] The royal commission was established by the federal government in June 1983 to "explore the most efficient, effective, and equitable means of promoting equality in employment for four groups: women, native people, disabled persons and visible minorities." It also analyzed the specific employment practices of eleven Crown corporations. The commission focused on policies and practices at the federal jurisdiction level and identified the following issues for immigrant professionals:

Many skilled and professional immigrants are frustrated by the absence of a mechanism to determine whether or not the professional qualifications they bring to this country qualify them to practise their profession in Canada or to determine what upgrading courses are necessary. The examinations and licensing requirements for many occupations and professions across Canada are prohibitively expensive. A system of qualification and credential assessment should be available so that recent as well as prospective immigrants can be advised accurately about exactly what is necessary in order to qualify them to practise their professions. It is a waste of human and intellectual resources that these people are consistently underemployed for reasons that have less to do with their professional qualifications or qualifiability and more to do with the insularity of some professional organizations. Having been selected as immigrants to Canada, many on the strength of these very qualifications, it is unfair to put insurmountable impediments in the way of their practising the professions they may be qualified to practice.[8]

Policies and practices of occupational regulatory bodies were also identified as barriers to immigrant professionals in the groundbreaking report, *Access! Task Force on Access to Professions and Trades in Ontario*.[9] The task force was struck in 1987 by the Ontario government to review the "rules and practices affecting entry to professions and trades to determine whether they have an actual or potential discriminatory effect on persons with training or experience from outside of Canada."[10] The task force identified barriers faced by immigrant professionals in regulated professions in Ontario, with professional credential recognition deemed to be the most significant. Other barriers highlighted include lack of clear information about professional standards and registration requirements, devaluation of international academic qualifications and experience, registration exams that do not demonstrate individuals' actual knowledge and skills, language tests that are too general and do not test occupation-specific terminology, lack of upgrading and bridge training opportunities and lack of internal appeals processes. Although the recommendations of the report were not implemented, possibly due to a change of government, the detailing of the barriers was an important development.

Other studies have shown that immigrant women of colour experience a dramatic disconnection between their experience, education and skill level and the occupations in which they find employment. Findings from a longitudinal study, *The Economic Integration of Immigrant Women in Toronto*, show that highly skilled immigrant women face severe occupational skidding in relocating in Canada. Of a sample size of 433 women, 65 percent had been working in professional jobs in their home country, 10 percent in managerial positions. After two years in Canada, only 29 percent of the women were working in professional jobs and 4 percent in management.[11] *The Facts Are In!*[12] reports similar results from a qualitative research project involving interviews with 643 immigrants (37.5 percent women) in regulated professions who immigrated to Ontario between 1994 and 1999. The research showed that fewer than 25 percent of the sample was working in their exact profession and that 47 percent were working in an unrelated field. At the time of the interviews, there were marked gender disparities in employment status. While 59 percent of the men were employed full-time, the rate for women was only 39 percent. The majority of women (56 percent) were either working part-time (17 percent) or not working (39 percent).

Devaluation of Credentials, Experience and Networks

When immigrants begin looking for a job in Canada, the first barrier they encounter is employers' lack of understanding of how their educational credentials and work experience relate to the Canadian context. In a survey of 2,091 employers conducted by Public Policy Forum,[13] researchers found that employers "overlook immigrants in their human resource planning, do not hire immigrants at the level at which they were trained, and face challenges integrating recent [less than ten years in Canada] immigrants into their workforce." While 39 percent of employers believed that "work experience from other countries was equal to Canadian work," on average 50 percent of the public, Crown corporations, non-profit and private companies surveyed indicated that "Canadian work experience was required" for employment and "Work experience from other countries was accepted but not necessarily considered equal to Canadian work."[14] Academic research supports this conclusion. Immigrants from non-traditional source countries are not credited for their years of international work experience when they are considered for jobs. Jeffrey Reitz points out:

> Canada's current immigration strategy rests largely on human capital theory. This theory was developed to increase our understanding of labour markets in a knowledge economy, but its weaknesses when applied to immigrants have become evident. Whereas human capital theory suggests that workers' earnings reflect the productive value of their skills — particularly skills based on formal education and work experience — immigrants' recent labour market outcomes contradict that expectation. Immigrants' skills have risen to unprecedented levels yet their earnings have fallen in both relative and absolute terms. Of immigrants arriving in 2000, for example, about 45 percent had university degrees yet their earnings after a year in Canada were less than those of previous comparable cohorts of immigrants going back to 1980.[15]

Since most employers devalue international work experience and do not draw on international academic assessment organizations to help them understand how an international degree compares with a Canadian degree, many immigrants are not fairly considered in job competitions. Further, these employers also devalue international professional contacts, such as previous employers of immigrants or international colleagues, when they insist on contacting a Canadian reference to speak about an applicant's work. Employers place great value on Canadian degrees and diplomas, Canadian work experience and Canadian references. The education and work experience that an immigrant is given points for in the immigration application do not readily translate into the workplace, and as a result "the best and the brightest" are treated as though they have no work history, no trustworthy references and questionable credentials.

Because of the devaluation of international credentials, experience and professional networks, getting "Canadian" work experience is the highest priority for immigrants. But this is not easy. Canadian work experience is consistently identified by immigrants as their biggest labour market barrier. The LSIC reported that "not enough Canadian work experience" was identified as the major barrier by 62.6 percent of newly arrived immigrants (in Canada for zero to six months), by 62.4 percent of recent immigrants (in Canada for seven to twenty-four months) as well as by 49.8 percent of immigrants with two to four years' tenure in Canada. Immigrants often ask, "How can I get Canadian experience if I can't get a job?" The persistent lack of Canadian work experience as a barrier to the labour market for immigrants raises questions about the nature of Canadian work experience itself. It is puzzling why immigrants who have been selected on the basis of their education, work experience and English and French language facility are unable to secure Canadian work experience four years after their arrival in Canada. As is evident from the immigration selection criteria, immigrants do not lack work experience. It is a basic fact, however, that immigrants do not have Canadian work experience when they first arrive in the country. Abella reported:

> Many immigrants find, too, that when they apply for employment they are told that the job requires Canadian experience, an impossible qualification for recently arrived immigrants.

Often the requirement has no objective relevance to the proper performance of the job.[16]

She recommended that "an employer's requirement of Canadian experience should be permitted only in those cases where it is demonstrated to be essential to the performance of the job."[17] Despite Abella's strong recommendation, Canadian work experience continues to be used by employers, nearly thirty years later, in a vague and undefined manner, and this forms a significant labour market barrier for immigrants.

For immigrants in regulated professions such as engineering, law, medicine and teaching, the impact of vaguely defined Canadian work experience requirements is severe; without Canadian work experience, professionals are not able to acquire a professional licence. The Policy Roundtable Mobilizing Professions and Trades (PROMPT), a community-based advocacy group focusing on employment issues for immigrant professionals and tradespeople, recommended that accessibility be considered a value in the registration processes of professional regulatory bodies. The group argues that to make the processes accessible it is necessary that

> the registration process does not include requirements that cannot reasonably be met by all qualified applicants. The onus is on the regulatory stakeholders to ensure that applicants have access to all elements of the licensing process/requirements that must be or can only be acquired in Canada.[18]

Employers and professional regulatory bodies need to clearly articulate what they mean by "Canadian experience." There have been challenges to the licensing processes of some professional regulatory bodies on the grounds that the one year of Canadian work experience requirements are not clearly outlined. For example, engineering graduates from Canadian universities have to have four years' work experience before they qualify for a professional licence, one of which has to be in Canada.[19] Immigrant engineers with years of international work experience, often with professional licences from their home countries, require one year of acceptable Canadian work experience for licensure. Cullingworth and Bambrah argue:

> The time has come to re-examine the idea of Canadian work experience and break down its components. As part of this re-examination, it's useful to review the historical context for including this requirement into the licensing process. Several questions then arise: Is this context still valid? Is one year of experience really essential to get exposure to Canadian engineering codes, legislation, technical standards and regulations? Could it be facilitated in different ways, or over other lengths of time? Could a mandatory course be offered to ensure that all applicants for licensing learn Canadian engineering codes, legislation, technical standards and regulations? Immigrant engineers who meet PEO's [Professional Engineers Ontario] requirements for four years of experience overall have already demonstrated their ability to apply the codes, regulations and standards from their country of training, and indeed multiple countries, into their work. All that is missing is knowledge that can be gained through classroom learning. These are questions that need to be considered.[20]

The processes used by regulatory bodies to assess and license internationally trained professionals varies from province to province and by profession. There are also a number of players involved including governments, professional organizations, regulatory bodies, educational institutions and community agencies, all of whom have developed specific procedures to recognize and assess the qualifications of immigrants. However, it has been pointed out that these procedures are often developed on an ad hoc basis with little coordination between the major players. For immigrants attempting to navigate this complex system of requirements and procedures, the process can be so cumbersome and difficult that many just give-up.[21] Furthermore, for many professions there remains a lack of independent appeals mechanisms for immigrants whose qualifications do get rejected.

Bridging programs, such as co-op placements or internships, to help immigrants get "Canadian work experience" can be scarce and difficult to access depending on immigrants' physical location and vocation. Many immigrants discover they need to return to school in Canada in order to get licensed in their profession, which can be both time-consuming and costly. Faced with the devaluation of their education, work experience and professional networks, immigrants often turn to survival jobs such as cleaning offices, driving taxis and labouring to make ends meet. While they are spending their time in these jobs that they are overqualified for, time passes, and it becomes increasingly difficult to get back into their profession. Often immigrants will offer to work for free, volunteering to get Canadian work experience. There is very little research on the effectiveness of volunteering as a strategy to enter the labour market. However, Schugurensky and Slade[22] found that the strategy of volunteering to gain appropriate work was only successful for a slim minority of the participants. At the time of their interviews, only 13 percent of participants were in a job that matched their skills and experience. Almost half of the participants were either underemployed (44 percent) or unemployed (42 percent). The research indicated that it is important for an immigrant to volunteer in the area of their skills and experience; taking unrelated volunteer work did not lead to appropriate paid work after the volunteer job was finished.

Impact of the Underemployment of Immigrants

The impact of the numerous labour market barriers facing immigrants in Canada is profound for immigrants and for the Canadian economy. It is critical to understand that the majority of immigrants to Canada since 1978 are from countries that were systematically discriminated against through formal immigration policy as recently as forty-three years ago. As more racialized immigrant professionals have migrated to Canada, the contradiction between recruiting immigrants for specific labour market needs and then not recognizing them for that work has intensified. Although explicitly race-based restrictions were removed from immigration policy in 1967, research has clearly demonstrated that racial discrimination has not been eliminated and people of colour, particularly women, are over-represented in low-paid, precarious jobs. This is especially pronounced when women are from non-English-speaking countries. According to Carol Goar, a reporter with the *Toronto Star*, "Although no one talks about skin colour, employers aren't hiring and promoting immigrants the way they did when most newcomers were white."[23] The legacy of racist immigration policies and practices seeking to create English Canada as a white British country are evident in the contemporary phenomenon of racialized poverty. Canada remains a society in which differences in skin colour or ethnic background continue to be important factors in determining one's life choices and chances.

It has been estimated that the Canadian economy loses between $4.1 and $15 billion annually due to lack of recognition of international educational credentials and work experience. According to the Conference Board of Canada:

> Canada would benefit by improving the openness and transparency of our learning and licensing organizations so that immigrants, especially, would feel that their expertise and credentials were properly appreciated and suitably recognized as having value. Given Canada's significant and increasing reliance on immigrant talent, it has to do a much better job of recognizing skills and learning that have been acquired in other countries.[24]

While the Conference Board of Canada rates the Canadian education system very highly (second only to Finland), it rates Canada's innovation, defined as "the ability to turn knowledge into new and improved goods and services" as a "D," ranking Canada fourteen out of seventeen countries. The innovation rating was the average of a twelve-point scale measuring such things as "trademarks per million population." One factor not mentioned in the Conference Board's analysis of Canada's performance is the deskilling of immigrants. Given that we recruit so many educated and experienced immigrants from all over the world, we should be a highly innovative and economically productive country. Allowing immigrants to enter jobs and professions that they are educated for and experienced in is both critical for the Canadian economy and for the well-being of individual immigrants who move to Canada in the hope of a good life. Immigrants are using food banks at an alarming rate. Removing unfair labour market barriers needs to be a priority for all levels of government.

4. THE RECEPTION PARTY
The Settlement Process for Immigrants

"Getting there is half the fun" an old saying goes. However, if you're a new immigrant in Canada, it's more likely that getting here was only "half the battle." Unfortunately, for most new immigrants, the second half of the battle begins when they hit Canadian soil. Though the promise of a new and better life in Canada is realized for many immigrants, the pathway is frequently fraught with many challenges. New immigrants face a host of settlement issues ranging from securing meaningful employment to improving language skills to accessing culturally appropriate health and social services. While settlement has always been an issue for immigrants arriving in Canada, recent immigrants face particular challenges with regard to their integration. Studies have documented that immigrants who arrived in Canada in the forty years proceeding World War II were able to participate in the labour market at the same level as Canadian-born citizens (usually within a year of their arrival) and that wage rates for these immigrants gradually rose to the same levels as well.[1] However, for immigrants arriving in Canada in the last twenty years, the story is very different. Even though these immigrants are more highly skilled and have higher education levels than their predecessors, they face considerable difficulties in finding jobs, especially in their fields. Ironically, as discussed in

> ### Canada's Track Record
>
> Canada's track record in successfully integrating immigrants is slipping. On average, immigrants arrive in this country better educated, in better health, and at similar stage of their careers as those born in the country, but the evidence suggests that during the past two decades, they have been much less successful in achieving success than earlier waves of immigration. Immigrants are having a harder time reaching Canadian income levels than was true in the past, in part because we have cut back on programs that help immigrants adjust and in part because many immigrants have difficulty gaining recognition for the education, skills and work experience they bring with them.
>
> Source: RBC in Sarah Wayland, *Unsettled: Legal and Policy Barriers for Newcomers to Canada* (Law Commission of Canada and Community Foundations of Canada, 2006).

Chapter 3, even though the immigration rules require high levels of skills and education in order to enter Canada, once here, many immigrants often never find jobs in their own field, and studies have shown how many others, especially immigrants of colour, face wage discrimination in their jobs.[2] Subsequently, many new immigrants and their families have to increasingly depend on social assistance programs, and rates of poverty are on the rise for this group of citizens in Canada.

In addition to the employment challenges and rising rates of poverty, recent immigrants face many other settlement obstacles, including difficulties with family reunification, finding appropriate housing, accessing language programs and navigating the Canadian health-care system. Settlement services, where they exist, may either not be known by new immigrants or easily accessed, due to their location, hours of operation or program limitations. While some may argue that settlement is an "immigrant" issue, the statistics show that immigrants are a part of Canada's social fabric — in fact, 18 percent of Canada's population was born overseas and immigration accounts for more than half of Canada's total population growth and 70 percent of the net growth in the labour market.[3] Furthermore, it is estimated that by 2016, 100 percent of the net growth in the labour market will come from immigrants.[4] Settlement can no longer be seen as an immigrant problem — rather, the barriers to settlement are increasingly being recognized as a Canadian societal problem that needs to be addressed by all levels of society — from government to non-profit agencies to the corporate sector to individuals. This chapter explores the issue of settlement, from how it is defined, to who is responsible to how services are organized, delivered and accessed. Lastly, we explore the settlement framework in Canada and whether it is fostering the social inclusion of new immigrants or whether it only serves to exacerbate their social exclusion.

What Is Settlement?

The term "settlement" has various definitions. According to Citizenship and Immigration Canada, settlement services consist of a variety of programs and services designed to help newcomers become participating members of Canadian society as quickly as possible. This official definition tends to view settlement as an immediate process; newly arrived immigrants have high priority needs such as shelter, employment and language training. Consequently, government-funded settlement services are geared towards serving these immediate needs. Others in the field, however, argue that while immigrants require these first-stop services, their needs do not necessarily end there. Intermediate and longer-term settlement services are also required to ensure that immigrants are fully able to participate in all facets of Canadian civic life. Intermediate needs could include things such as employment-specific language and skills training (though many advocates argue that these should also be included as an "immediate need") and longer-term housing needs or assistance with accessing the legal system. Longer-term requirements could consist of political and civic education. The current settlement system, however, is primarily geared to providing solely for the immediate physical and social needs of new immigrants when they arrive in Canada. These needs can be categorized into four major areas: employment, language training, health and housing.

Employment

Finding appropriate employment is frequently the first concern of new immigrants arriving in Canada. Given that Canada's primary channel of immigration (the Skilled Worker Class) focuses on immigrants who have high levels of education, skill and language abilities and that priority is given to migrants who fall into one of the twenty-nine priority occupations, many immigrants believe that finding a job in Canada will be fairly easy. That belief, however, rapidly changes. As discussed extensively in Chapter 3, many immigrants discover that their education and work experience are not recognized by Canadian employers. In addition to lack of skills' recognition, immigrants face a host of other employment related issues. First of all, even while still in their home country, there is often a lack of accurate information regarding working in Canada. While the promise of plentiful jobs may lure immigrants to Canada, by the time they arrive, the situation may have changed in their employment field. Second, while language skills is one of the criteria used to grant immigrant status, these skills may not be sufficient to work in specific fields. Occupational-specific language training is often needed so immigrants can become acquainted with Canadian terminology. Workplace cultures and practices also vary across countries, and new immigrants may be unfamiliar with Canadian norms. Lastly, immigrants may face discrimination in the Canadian labour market and may not know of or have access to legal help to challenge discriminatory practices. All of these factors contribute to the challenges of finding appropriate employment, and consequently, unlike in the past, when immigrant earnings converged with those of native-born Canadians after several years, the earnings of the most recent wave of immigrants may never reach the levels of their Canadian-born counterparts.

The impact of these obstacles not only affects immigrants and their families, but the wider Canadian society loses out on the experience and knowledge of highly skilled immigrants. In the meantime, immigrants suffer the economic, social and health consequences of not being able to find gainful employment, including increased stress, poverty and social isolation.

Language Training

Language education encompasses many different facets and levels. While immigrants who arrive in Canada frequently have some ability in English or French, they may not be proficient enough to find work or communicate easily with other English/French speakers. It has been shown that employment earnings increase with language competency, and certainly, the degree of proficiency in one of Canada's official languages will affect immigrants' ability to participate in all aspects of Canadian civic life. Children of immigrants also face challenges if they cannot communicate fluently in either English or French, and they can be left behind academically because of linguistic challenges. In fact, high drop-out rates for immigrant youth have been linked to language difficulties in school.[5]

Finding appropriate language training courses can be challenging for new immigrants. While the federal government funds a program entitled Language Instruction for Newcomers to Canada (LINC), it is not offered in all provinces. British Columbia, Manitoba and Quebec control their own language instruction programs. Furthermore, LINC programs tend to be available primarily in larger urban areas, and depending on the city, programs may only be offered up to a certain level and then usually for a fixed time period (four years is the maximum, though typically, most immigrants use LINC for about a year). Provinces and school boards are responsible for funding language training in schools, but these too can vary across cities and school boards, and teaching ESL is not part of teacher training in any province. Access to LINC programs is limited to permanent residents or Convention refugees. Temporary immigrants, non-status immigrants, refugee claimants and Canadian citizens cannot access federally funded LINC programs (or any other federal settlement programs).

Health Care

Health care is an integral part of the settlement process. Studies have shown that when immigrants first arrive in Canada, they are generally in better health than their Canadian-born counterparts of comparable age.[6] The reasons for this are many, including the mandatory medical screenings immigrants undergo before being given permission to immigrate. However, once in Canada, immigrants' overall health deteriorates over time, especially for those arriving from non-European countries. Part of this can be linked to immigrants' lack of use of the Canadian health-care system, particularly mental and preventative health-care services. The Longitudinal Study of Immigrants to Canada revealed that only 19 percent of immigrants had accessed health-care services during their first six months in Canada. There can be a number of reasons for the underutilization of health-care services. Lack of knowledge of services available, linguistic challenges or fear of health concerns being passed on to immigration officials may all contribute to im-

---

Health Coverage

A recent study by Dr. Paul Caulford, Chief of Family Medicine at Scarborough Hospital (profiled in Sylvain 2005) found that tens of thousands of immigrants and refugees in Canada may lack any kind of health coverage. The study found two main groups of uninsured patients: (1) those waiting to clear a mandatory three-month waiting period for provincial coverage, and (2) those pursuing a claim for residency status. Other patients were either in Canada without status or of "precarious status," e.g., in Canada on a temporary residence permit. Based on extrapolation from existing data, Caulford estimated that Ontario alone could have at least 50,000 uninsured immigrants and refugees.

Source: Sarah Wayland, *Unsettled: Legal and Policy Barriers for Newcomers to Canada: Literature Review* (Law Commission of Canada and Community Foundations of Canada, 2006) p. 103.

migrants not accessing health care. For others, the reasons may be more structural. In Ontario, Quebec, British Columbia and New Brunswick — provinces that receive close to 90 percent of all immigrants — immigrants must wait three months before being covered by provincial health coverage. This period begins once immigrants are granted permanent residency status. It is estimated that, at any given time, there are tens of thousands of immigrants, refugees and other non-status immigrants who are living without provincial health coverage (see Box: Health Coverage).

Housing

Adequate housing (along with employment) is probably one of the biggest challenges of settlement for new immigrants. Housing can affect an immigrant's access to schools and services, their quality of life and their ability to tap into an extended social network. According the Canadian Mortgage and Housing Corporate survey in 2001, 18.3 percent of immigrants were living in unacceptable housing conditions. This percentage was significantly higher (36 percent) for recent immigrants, as well as those living in urban areas. A number of factors can affect housing choices, including a lack of affordable housing, high rental costs, discrimination in the housing market, a lack of knowledge around tenant rights and linguistic challenges. Inadequate housing can lead to higher housing costs, resulting in less money for other necessities such as food, medicine and clothing.

Addressing Settlement Issues

Addressing the settlement issues of new immigrants requires many approaches. Different levels of government fund a number of initiatives to provide immigrants with the information and services they need once they arrive in Canada. From information booklets to immigration websites to ethno-specific organizations to large multi-service settlement agencies, it would seem that immigrants have a plethora of options when it comes to addressing their needs.

However, a closer look at these initiatives shows some serious gaps.

With regard to accessing settlement information prior to entering Canada, immigrants could turn to the internet, which provides general resources, as well as guides to settlement issues in Canada. However, there are a number of limitations regarding internet resources. First of all, most of the electronic resources listed are only available in English and occasionally in French and are thus completely inaccessible to those who do not speak or have proficiency in one of the two official languages. These resources, which include both province-specific guides and general settlement issues, can be difficult to locate electronically. A cursory examination of these different guides also reveals varying levels of information, from very general information on obtaining work, housing and health care, to more specific information on Canadian cultural norms. Both the guidebooks and general websites, however, tend to assume a "one size fits all" approach to settlement, in that the information does not address that immigrants come from a range of cultures, languages, classes and immigrant experiences. For example, an English-speaking Business Class immigrant would have different settlement needs than a non-English skilled tradesperson or a Live-In Caregiver. Thus, the ways in which they would each access areas such as housing and employment could be completely different.

Once in Canada, new immigrants can access a wider range of resources, including federally funded language programs (such as LINC) and the Immigrant Settlement and Adaptation Program, both of which are available through a variety of multi-service settlement organizations and ethno-specific agencies. These organizations usually provide more specific services in a variety of languages. However, access to these organizations is predicated on a number of factors, such as an immigrant's awareness of the agencies, where they have settled in Canada, transport, including public transportation, and their time availability. If immigrants live in rural areas or do not have extensive social networks, access to and/or awareness of these services can be limited. Similarly, the times in which the programs are offered may not be suitable given job or childcare responsibilities.

For immigrants who are lucky enough to live in urban areas, have an awareness of the settlement programs available to them and have the time and transport to attend programs, chances are that the available support and information will only assist them with the first phase of settlement in Canada. As noted earlier, most funders (both government and private) tend to only fund the first stage of settlement, which addresses immediate housing, language and employment needs. But as advocates, immigrants and scholars argue, settlement must be seen as a process rather than an activity of immigration. Moreover, the settlement process and immigrants' subsequent needs vary depending on race, class, family status and channels of immigration. While social services, settlement agencies and ethno-specific agencies attempt to meet these various needs, their own mandates are hampered by shrinking funding and a political climate that does not always reflect the realities that new immigrants face. As a result, in contrast to being a new land of opportunities, immigrants' experience in Canada often becomes that of obstacles and challenges to finding work, housing and appropriate services.

How Settlement Services Work

Settlement agencies provide a range of programs and services, from language classes to employment training to information about how to access social services. The location of settlement agencies tends to mirror immigration patterns to Canada. Given that immigration tends to be an urban phenomenon, with over 70 percent of immigrants settling in Toronto, Montreal and Vancouver, and over half arriving in Toronto alone, it is no coincidence that the majority of settlement services are concentrated in those three cities. Cities outside this immigrant corridor may not have any ethno-specific agencies, and it may be up to larger multi-ethnic and multi-service agencies to serve a variety of populations. For immigrants living in rural areas, there may be no settlement agencies at all, and accessing any language, employment or information services may entail a trip to an urban centre, possibly a significant distance away.

In Canada, settlement services are provided primarily by a network of non-profit agencies funded mainly by different levels of government, although other sources of funding include the private sector and foundations. In order to illustrate how these agencies work, Beyene[7] identifies three main service-delivery models involved in providing settlement services to immigrants in Canada: a) mainstream, b) multi-cultural and c) ethno-specific. According to Beyene, mainstream agencies tend to be large organizations that provide services to the general population. In order to access funds for settlement services, they may hire bilingual service workers, access cross-cultural training for their existing staff or attempt outreach to ethnic communities. However, these agencies have been criticized for lacking culturally and linguistically appropriate services and for having a Euro-centric orientation and poor connections to ethno-specific agencies. Multi-cultural agencies are able to counter some of these issues, given that their mandate is to serve particular cultural communities; however, they may still assume a "one size fits all" approach when dealing with specific ethnic populations. While ethno-specific agencies may solve all these problems, of the three models, these tend to be small, under-staffed, under-funded and run mainly by volunteers.[8] While Beyene's summary provides a useful overview of the organization and delivery of settlement services, the reality is often much more complicated. For example, larger mainstream agencies may be located in and well connected to the local ethnic communities, and some immigrants may prefer to go to larger community organizations in order to ensure their anonymity. Furthermore, not all ethno-specific organizations represent the diversity of their populations, and there may be political or social issues that keep some people from accessing these agencies.

Settlement agencies are funded through service agreements negotiated by the federal government with individual provinces. Since these agreements vary by province, the funding of agencies and level of service also varies. For example, the agreement signed between Ontario and the federal government resulted in a large injection of funds to settlement agencies over the last few years. Settlement agencies access government funds primarily through program-specific grants and purchase-of-service agreements (such as LINC programs). In addition to the government funds (which are accessed through the federal, provincial and municipal levels), many agencies also rely on foundations and other private endeavours. One of the consequences of these various funding sources is that funding is fragmented and staff time is being redirected from direct service provision to grant writing and evaluation reports. Fundraising and seeking collaborative partnerships are two other activities that use up valuable staff resources as agencies attempt to gather funds from private donors and charitable foundations or work with other agencies to provide necessary settlement services. While on the surface, diversifying funding sources and working with other agencies may appear to be positive consequences, the reality is that they often increase the administrative function of agencies. More staff time is devoted to managing and accounting for funds to the several different donors, while collaboration between agencies often results in smaller ethnospecific agencies being dependent on larger multi-service agencies that are able to secure collaborative contracts.[9]

Is Settlement Working?

Settlement services in Canada constitute a large and complicated labyrinth of funding, programs and service providers. The disparity in funding across provinces and in municipalities, along with the concentration of immigrants in certain major urban centres, also adds to the intricate web of services across Canada. All these factors affect the type and extent of programs and services that are offered in cities and towns. Add to this the changing face and needs of immigrants themselves and one can understand the challenges of providing settlement services across the country. The question, however, remains — is settlement working? And perhaps, more importantly, for whom is it working?

Immigrants, as has been illustrated throughout this book, are not a homogenous category. For example, not all immigrants will require or access settlement services. But for those who need them, and statistics show that there is a growing number of immigrants from source countries such as Africa, Asia and Latin America, settlement services are an integral part of integrating into life in Canada. In addition to potential language needs, accessing employment is often the primary concern of new immigrants to Canada. The reality is that the lack of international credential recognition and the requirement for Canadian work experience are the two biggest barriers to getting a job. Settlement agencies, while providing employment services such as resume preparation, interview techniques and even potential intern placements, cannot overcome this one huge obstacle, which requires a major policy overhaul on the parts of both governments and industries.

The channels through which immigrants arrive and stay in Canada are changing. The largest category of immigrants who arrive in Canada is now low-skilled temporary workers who come here for a particular time period into a specified job (see Table 5.1 in Chapter 5). While these immigrants may not technically "settle" in Canada, they still pay federal and provincial taxes and live in communities, often for the majority of a year, year after year. And while temporary immigrant workers may not need employment or even housing assistance (many temporary workers are provided housing as part of their work arrangement), they may be in desperate need of information and advocacy regarding labour and human rights — two areas that are not currently included in the government definition of settlement services. Lastly, non-status immigrants have no recourse to settlement services even though they provide critical labour in many industries facing labour shortages, including the construction industry and as live-in caregivers, and they pay taxes.

Settlement agencies have had to change the way they operate, with the fragmented funding avenues, devoting valuable staff time to writing grants and evaluation reports and frequently losing valuable programs such as advocacy, employment equity and anti-racism initiatives which are not longer covered by grants. In addition, many smaller ethno-specific agencies have been forced to shut their doors altogether or merge and/or partner with larger agencies in order to provide ethno and linguistic specific services.[10] More importantly, the focus of programs and services in these agencies remains the immediate needs of immigrants when they first arrive. Intermediate and longer-term issues for immigrants such as employment specific language training or information on or access to Canada's health or legal system remain outside the purview of most settlement agencies. Lastly, the location of settlement agencies as well as the structure of their programs frequently have a huge impact on access. Are the agencies accessible by public transport? Are there transportation subsidies (e.g., bus or subway tickets)? Are programs and services offered in the evening hours? Is childcare available? These critical issues define exactly who can access settlement services and perhaps for how long. With increasing rates of poverty among new immigrant populations, the answers to the above questions determine just who can access settlement services and for how long.

All these issues point to a system that clearly can be improved to meet the diverse settlement needs of all immigrants that arrive and stay in Canada. From policy and funding changes at the government level that allow agencies to provide for the diversity and breadth of issues affecting immigrants today, to a wider network of agencies, including ethno-specific agencies under the settlement umbrella, we can have a settlement framework that truly responds to and strives to integrate all immigrants.

Conclusion

All the players involved in the settlement field have some way to go in addressing the diversity of immigrants coming into Canada and the range and depth of their needs. From government funding to industry training and accreditation, to a larger definition of what constitutes settlement and the time it takes to become an active social citizen, changes need to be made at all levels. Immigrants are a critical aspect of Canada's social fabric; they bring with them important skills, experience, knowledge and culture, which all contribute to what it means to be Canadian. They also pay taxes, buy consumer goods and services and contribute to the overall growth and sustenance of the Canadian economy. Consequently, the adequate funding and delivery of settlement services should be prioritized as an essential right as opposed to an issue that is vulnerable to the particular political inclinations of various governments. Similar to education and health care, while not all people may access these services, the government and Canadians recognize that they are important social areas to be properly funded and supported; they provide for the growth and well-being of Canada as a whole. Settlement services should be treated in the same manner. With almost one-fifth of Canadians coming from other countries, their settlement and integration into Canadian life similarly provides for the continued growth and well-being of Canada and ensures that Canada retains its reputation for being a fair, welcoming and accepting nation.

5. THE REVOLVING DOOR
Temporary Workers in Canada

Every year Canada brings in tens of thousands of immigrants to be employed as temporary foreign workers. The government of Canada defines a temporary foreign worker as

> temporary residents who entered Canada mainly to work and have been issued a work permit (with or without other types of permits). A work permit is an official document issued by an officer that allows someone who is not a Canadian citizen or a permanent resident to work in Canada. Some temporary jobs in Canada may not require a work permit—for example, news reporters, public speakers, performing artists, foreign government officers. For statistical purposes, a temporary resident is designated as foreign worker on the basis of our determination of his or her "yearly status"—the main reason for which the person has been authorized to enter and stay temporarily in Canada during the year of observation.[1]

Following on the heels of both Europe and the United States, Canada is witnessing an explosion in temporary foreign workers. The latest figures reveal that over 270,000 immigrants came to Canada on temporary permits in 2008.[2] Besides the sheer number of immigrants coming to Canada through this channel, never before have temporary immigrants outnumbered immigrants from all categories entering Canada as permanent residents (see Table 5.1).

Temporary foreign workers are hired in a number of fields. Some are admitted through specific programs geared to particular industries, such as agricultural workers (Seasonal Agricultural Worker Program) and caregivers (Live-In Caregiver Program). For employment categories not covered by specific programs, individual employers must go through a lengthy process to bring in temporary workers. Regardless of whether the migrants come through a program or through an individual petition, Canadian employers must provide proof that there are no Canadians available to complete the work offered to temporary foreign workers. This is because the main goal of these temporary labour programs is to meet the labour needs in industries where there is a shortage of Canadians to perform the tasks.

Table 5.1 Numbers of Immigrants Admitted to Canada in 2008, by Category

Immigrant Category	Admitted	
	Number	Percent
Total Economic Class (including dependants)	149,072	60.3
Total Family Class	65,567	26.5
Total Protected Persons	21,860	8.8
Total others	10,742	4.3
Category not stated	2	0.0
Total number of immigrants admitted as permanent residents	247,243	100
Total Students	79,536	29.2
Total Temporary Workers	192,373	70.8
Total number of temporary immigrants admitted	271,909	100

Source: Citizenship and Immigration Canada, "Facts and Figures 2009 — Immigration Overview: Permanent and Temporary Residents," at <cic.gc.ca/english/resources/statistics/facts2009/index.asp> (2010).

The move towards allowing migrants to fill seasonal or periodical employment needs is said to offer new opportunities for immigrants, employers and the Canadian government. For the labour migrants, it provides a structured, legal framework for entering and working in Canada. Temporary programs allow companies to fulfill immediate labour shortages without having to hire permanent workers. For the Canadian government, foreign worker permits provide a way to "fill labour shortages in Canada and bring new skills and knowledge to help the country's economy grow"[3] and usually without any long-term commitments to providing citizenship and all its attendant rights and privileges. But who are these programs being marketed to? Where are the majority of temporary workers coming from? Are these programs really all that advantageous to workers? And, is there a connection between the "temporariness" in these programs and the workers who are coming through these programs? This chapter examines the growth of these programs in Canada with a focus on the Seasonal Agricultural Worker Program to show how temporary labour programs in Canada are creating a new underclass of labourers and citizens.

History of Temporary Foreign Workers in Canada

Canada's employment of foreign workers has a long and troubled history. From the building of the railroad to working in sawmills to domestic work, Canada has relied on foreign workers to fill the labour gap when Canadian workers were unable or unwilling to do certain types of work. The migration of foreign workers into Canada can be traced back to the late nineteenth century, when the first Chinese labourers arrived to work on the railroads. During the late 1800s, Canada authorized thousands of Chinese migrants to build the train tracks from British Colombia to Thunder Bay (see Chapter 2). Once the tracks were built, many of the workers were expelled, and for those who remained, an exorbitant head tax made it almost impossible to bring over their wives and families. While Chinese immigration marks one of the first entry points of foreign workers into Canada, it wasn't until the early twentieth century that the Canadian government began to formally permit foreign temporary workers. Initiated in 1910, the Caribbean domestic scheme brought in a hundred women from Guadeloupe to Quebec to fill the labour shortages in domestic work. Although Canada also imported scores of women from Europe during this period for similar purposes, the European women filled a dual purpose in their immigration to Canada. Women from the British Isles were also brought in to become wives of British men stationed in Canada; thus they came to Canada as permanent immigrants. Caribbean women on the other hand worked for a specific period and then they were sent back, despite the ongoing shortage of domestic workers. This exclusionary policy for domestic workers based on country of origin meant that from 1904 to 1931, only 2,363 Caribbean women were imported as domestic workers.[4]

Foreign migration into Canada was severely curtailed during the 1930s and part of the 1940s, with the Canadian government effectively banning all contract labour programs (the source of foreign temporary labour) until the after World War II.[5] In 1947, the government lifted the ban, and 4,527 Polish ex-servicemen came to Canada as "qualified agriculturists." Although the program was framed as a temporary work program, the migrants were granted landed immigrant status upon arrival.[6] The 1950s also saw the reintroduction of the program aimed at bringing domestic workers from the Caribbean. Unlike the 1910 program, these Caribbean women arrived as landed immigrants. However, even with granted landed immigrant status, the Canadian government retained the right to deport these women if they were found to be "undesirable" by becoming pregnant or severing their contract with their employer. It is interesting to note that many of the women who came to Canada through this channel were highly skilled as nurses, teachers and civil servants, yet the government expected that they would continue to work as domestics beyond their one-year contract because of a perceived notion that Black women were "naturally" suited to domestic work.[7]

It wasn't until the mid 1960s that the Canadian government formally introduced its first temporary work program aimed at bringing in agricultural workers from Jamaica. The Seasonal Agricultural Worker Program (SAWP) was introduced by the Department of Labour in 1966 to alleviate the labour shortages facing Ontario agricultural growers. In its first year, 264 Jamaican workers entered Canada via this program, which was expanded to Trinidad and Tobago and Barbados the following year and then to other Caribbean countries in 1973. In 1974, the program was expanded to include migrants from Mexico. Unlike earlier labour contract programs, this was the first program that did not grant workers landed immigrant status. Instead, migrant workers were brought to Canada to work on farms for a specified period of time, after which they returned to their countries of origin.

In 1973, this initial labour contract program was expanded to include other spheres of employment, including domestic work, with the introduction of the Non-Immigrant Employment Authorization Program (NIEAP). This program operated similarly to the SAWP in that migrants were admitted into the country to perform a specific form of labour for a designated period of time. As part of the NIEAP, employers had to demonstrate that there were no Canadians available for the specified employment. Migrants admitted under the program had to adhere to a number of conditions as part of their contract, including not being able to change their employer without permission and, frequently, living in housing provided by the employer. Domestic workers in particular were hard hit as they were no longer admitted as landed immigrants and would be sent home after their period of employment. These restrictive rules have often led to oppressive working conditions, and some advocates argue that temporary workers are a form of "unfree" labour. They are deemed unfree because many migrants will stay in dangerous or exploitative jobs without complaining because they fear not being able to return for future periods of seasonal employment. Furthermore, this lack of freedom is cemented through the multiple restrictions placed on migrants while in Canada, from their lack of choice in housing and employment to the potential isolation they may experience while living in their employers' homes, with little access to public transportation.

Despite these restrictive conditions, the number of migrants entering through the NIEAP has increased exponentially over the last thirty years. While over 69,000 migrant workers entered in 1973 through this category, by 1980, this number had increased to over 98,000, and by 1990, over 165,000 migrants entered into Canada as temporary workers. While the NIEAP does include a range of different employments, a substantial portion of migrants entering through this category come for domestic work and seasonal farming.[8] In contrast to the labour migrants from the past, who originated in Europe (and who were granted landed immigrant status upon entry), overwhelmingly, these new domestic and farm workers came from the less economically developed countries in the Global South (e.g., the Philippines, Mexico, the Caribbean). Thus, as Canada shifted its policies to accommodate more migrants from the Global South, there was a corresponding shift in immigration policy that dictated that these migrations be temporary and linked to work that was often low-paid, low-skilled and with few labour protections. This trend continues today with temporary foreign workers making up the largest single category of migration into Canada. The following section explores how contemporary temporary worker programs are organized, the inequalities between different types of programs and how certain categories of migrant workers are made "unfree."

Temporary Foreign Workers Today

Currently, employers from any number of employment fields can petition the government to hire a temporary foreign worker. The process they follow typically involves submitting an application to

Human Resources and Social Development Canada (HRSDC) for the position. The government then considers the application with regard to the following criteria:

- the job offer is genuine;
- the wages and working conditions are comparable to those offered to Canadians working in the occupation;
- employers conducted reasonable efforts to hire or train Canadians for the job;
- the foreign worker is filling a labour shortage;
- the employment of the foreign worker will directly create new job opportunities or help retain jobs for Canadians;
- the foreign worker will transfer new skills and knowledge to Canadians; and
- the hiring of the foreign worker will not affect a labour dispute or the employment of any Canadian worker involved in such a dispute.

Once the employer's application is approved, the foreign worker must apply for a work permit in their country of residence.

In addition to this generic process, the government has created special criteria if hiring foreign workers from the following six employment fields: academia, seasonal agriculture, film and entertainment, information technology, live-in caregiving, and a pilot program for occupations requiring lower levels of formal training. Each employment designation comes with its particular skills requirement and application procedures. While some are brief, others involve substantial memorandums of understanding, while others encompass lengthy files.

A comparison of two employment categories reveals some interesting differences. The Information Technology Program, for example, requires no confirmation letter from HRSDC; thus, a worker's permit may get processed more quickly. In addition, there are no living requirements, no time limits and no long contracts outlining itemized details of work; the application procedure is relatively simple and brief. Moreover, should the applicant decide to apply for citizenship, they would score highly on the points-based system required for landed immigrant status created by Citizenship and Immigration Canada (CIC). On the other hand, the Seasonal Agricultural Worker Program entails a rather more cumbersome admission procedure. Once the employers receive approval from HRSDC, applicants have to endure a long process before being accepted into the program. First, they must apply in person to the Ministry of Labour in their home country. Second, recruitment into the program is based on a number of factors, including prior agricultural experience and more importantly, that the applicant be in need of financial assistance. If accepted into the program, agricultural workers have significantly less options than their information technology counterparts. They must live in housing provided by their employers and some even have their meals supplied. They can also only work for a maximum of eight months. Furthermore, workers have little rights or say in determining who they will work for, where they will live or even their own mobility while in Canada. Lastly, if agricultural workers should desire any form of permanent residency in Canada, the CIC criteria would make it near impossible for workers to meet the minimum requirements.[9]

These two brief examples show that Canada, although experiencing a shortage of both information technology workers and seasonal agricultural workers, sets up two very different processes for workers from each of these categories. Highly skilled workers have an easier time applying to the program, more flexibility with their work contracts and greater choices regarding their lifestyle while in Canada. The Information Technology Program even has provisons for bringing applicants' spouses. The Seasonal Agricultural Worker Program has no such choice or flexibility, and there is absolutely no provision for accompanying family members, even though the majority of participants in this program are married with several children.[10] While there are no statistics that capture country of origin for temporary foreign workers in the Information Technology Program, we do know that workers in the Mexican and Caribbean Seasonal Agricultural Worker Program must come from countries that fall in the Global South — Mexico, Jamaica and other Caribbean countries — as the name of the program indicates.

When turning to the statistics on countries of origin for temporary foreign workers, another interesting story emerges. While the U.S. is the largest single sending country for foreign workers, their numbers have fallen radically in the last ten years, from 41,911 in 1999 to 31,399 in 2008.[11] During the same time, the second and third largest migrant sending countries have experienced dramatic surges in the number of workers coming to Canada: Mexico sent 8,118 workers in 1999 and 20,900 in 2008, and the Philippines sent 2,225 in 1999 and 19,253 in 2008. In fact, Mexico and the Philippines combined sent more temporary migrant workers to Canada than the U.S.[12] Now let's correlate those numbers with the number of foreign workers entering into the Seasonal Agricultural Worker Program and the Live-In Caregiver Program. The Seasonal Agricultural Worker Program brought 21,328 workers into Canada in 2008,[13] while the Live-In Caregiver Program had 34,462[14] applicants coming to Canada. We can safely assume that the majority of migrants coming from the Philippines are probably heading towards the Live-In Caregiver Program, while the majority of Mexican migrants are destined for the Seasonal Agricultural Worker Program. These are two of the most regulated of programs in the temporary workers category, as well as the two spheres of employment that are contributing to the growth of unfree labour in Canada. The next section examines how one of these programs, the Mexican Seasonal Agricultural Worker Program, creates unfree labour.

Case Study 1: The Mexican Seasonal Agricultural Worker Program

Since 1974, the Mexican Seasonal Agricultural Worker Program (MSAWP) has been providing Canadian farms, especially those located in Ontario, with rural Mexican workers. The program is administered by a federally appointed government agency, the Foreign Agricultural Resource Management Services (FARMS). FARMS, together with federal counterparts in Mexico — the Ministry of External Relations, the Ministry of Interior, the Ministry of Labour and Social Planning and the Ministry of Health, as well as Mexican consulates in Canada — work with Canadian agricultural growers to recruit, hire and transport Mexican workers to Canadian farms.[15]

In order to recruit foreign seasonal agricultural workers, Canadian farmers first have to demonstrate to their local HRSDC office at least eight weeks in advance of any recruitment that there is an inadequate supply of Canadian labour to fulfill agricultural tasks. The HRSDC assesses the availability of qualified workers as well as the growers' employment history with regards to recruitment and retention of employees. If the request is approved, growers are matched up with approved participants from Mexico. For Mexicans applying for the program, the process to be approved as a foreign seasonal agricultural worker takes a little longer.

One of the first steps potential Mexican applicants must undertake is to travel to the capital, Mexico City, to apply in person at the Ministry of Labour. This travel requirement already deters many Mexicans from applying, especially if they live a great distance away. Ministry officials ascertain that the applicant has prior agricultural experience and more importantly, that they are in need of financial assistance. In other words, the best-suited applicants are those who are landless, who lack other avenues for employment and who have the lowest levels of education. Applicants must even submit official letters confirming their *campesino* (peasant) status.[16] In addition, Ministry officials tend to favour applicants who are over twenty-five (although eighteen is the minimum age for participation in the program), are married and have large families. These last factors help ease the worries of Canadian immigration authorities, whose prevailing fear is that seasonal workers may want to become permanent residents. Women are infrequently accepted into the program because this would require Canadian growers to provide separate housing for them.[17]

Workers who have prior experience in the MSAWP may be requested by growers. According to FARMS, over 70 percent of the Mexicans participating in the program have been named by their employers.[18] Although this process is advantageous in many respects for Mexicans participating in the program, it does limit the possibilities for new workers to join. In addition, it leaves the active participants vulnerable to the growers' exploitation, since they are dependent on a positive review in order to be "named" by their employers. One other factor regulating workers' behaviour and subsequent return in the following season is the review that employers are asked to write for each of the participants. Each Mexican participant, upon returning home, is required to report to the Ministry of Labour and hand in their evaluation, as well as provide an account of their expenses while in Canada. The Ministry official tallies the worker's expenses in order to ensure that Canadian-earned wages were not spent frivolously by workers or their families.[19] These forms of surveillance and regulation of Mexican participants severely curtail workers' rights and freedoms.

Once in Canada, Mexican migrant workers' lives are governed by a strict set of regulations that determines where they will live, when they will eat, sometimes even what they will eat and how much leisure time they can have. There are also harsh restrictions on where they can spend their leisure time, given their physical isolation on rural farms. They have no say regarding their employer, their housing, who they are housed with or how their work days and work weeks are structured. Migrant workers must contribute to federal tax programs, including Employment Insurance (EI) and pension programs, but many of them will never see any long-term benefits to their investment. Although migrant workers may be entitled to some of these benefits, such as parental leave or pension benefits, many are unaware of their rights or the process involved to receive them. Moreover, some Employment Insurance benefits are denied altogether. For example, migrant workers are not qualified for lay-off benefits because of their non-citizenship status, despite the fact that they pay the same EI premiums as other workers. Migrant workers are also not allowed to unionize. Migrant workers rarely take any sick leave, even when injured, and few protest or question their participation in the use of harmful pesticides. The reasons for migrant workers' compliance in these conditions are usually twofold: because many of them come from poor rural families in Mexico, the Canadian currency they receive in exchange for their work is more than they could ever make in Mexico, where the daily wage is often $1 to $2. Second, migrant workers are completely dependent on their employers' good evaluation and their "named request" in order to return to Canada the following season. But these conditions are just the beginning of the story of migrant agricultural work in Canada. To actually understand how migrant workers live and contribute to our Canadian lifestyle, let's examine the politics of "local food."

Case Study 2: The Untold Tale of Local Food

The politics of local food has been touted as a way to sustain our economy, support our farmers and keep agriculture alive in Canada. While there are many virtues of eating local, next time you bite into your local strawberry, tear off a lettuce leaf or slice into a red ripe tomato, ask yourself, how did it get to your plate? What kind of labour went into planting that fruit, monitoring its growth and harvesting it? The answer is not as rosy as we would like to believe. Researchers and migrant advocates have uncovered exploitative labour and living conditions that are often the hidden face of the local food movement. Workers describe living eight to ten people deep in one room, with only one bathroom, others have described housing that even lacks bedding. During harvest times, workers are often pressured to work seven days a week, ten to twelve hours a day, since harvesting is done on a tight schedule. Agricultural work may also involve working with harmful pesticides, and workers have testified that they were asked to do so without any formal training or protection.[20] Leisure time, when it occurs, is also carefully structured and monitored. Given that most migrant workers live in rural areas, they are dependent on their employer to drive them into the nearest town in order to buy provisions, which is often done only once a week. In interviews conducted with migrant workers in Simcoe, Ontario,[21] workers spoke of the three to four hour window they were given to do their groceries, errands, doctors' visits or any other leisure activity. Buses would come into the main shopping centre parking lot and hundreds of migrant workers would fill grocery stores, fast food outlets, restaurants and the occasional bar. Ironically, interviews conducted with local residents revealed how most stayed away from the downtown core during the migrant worker nights.

The United Food and Commercial Workers Union, which has been advocating on behalf of and working to unionize agricultural workers, highlights the oppressive contracts that Guatemalan migrant workers are forced to sign, drafted by the Canadian agri-business employer group FERME and, even more surprisingly, an intergovernmental agency that is supposed to advocate for migrants — the International Organization for Migration, which include provisions such as:

- During your stay in Canada, you should only do the activities you are assigned to and should not distract yourself with any group or association;
- Reasons to exclude you from the program that will force you to pay your plane ticket: alcoholism, theft, lack of respect and sexual relations;
- Upon arrival at the farm, the employer will keep your passport for the duration of your stay in Canada;

- Use deodorant before the flight and every day you stay in Canada;
- Beware of having relations with women;
- In case you needed to go back to Guatemala before ending your contract, you will have to prove that you have a good reason. Even then, the employer can choose whether to hire you the next season;
- You should keep your hair short to avoid lice.[22]

These conditions are what contribute to the "unfreedom" of migrant workers. Moreover, because agricultural work is largely invisible, both geographically (out in rural farms) and in our framing of local food (the movement and the media frequently frames local food as the product of hardworking, primarily white, farm families), their unfreedom never enters the public debate around agriculture in Canada. And while migrant workers are paid for their work in Canada, as are all foreign temporary workers, no other temporary worker program, except the Live-In Caregiver Program, places so many restrictions on its workers. And unlike the Live-In Caregiver Program, migrant agricultural workers are ineligible for Canadian citizenship, regardless of whether they have been in Canada for two years or twenty years. Instead they are placed on a merry-go-round of seasonal work, which has them in Canada for eight months of the year, year after year. It's no wonder that some workers joke about "vacationing in Mexico." By creating a class of ongoing temporary workers, the Canadian government collects valuable tax dollars, doesn't have to provide many of the benefits and rights accorded to citizens and ensures that the needs of the agricultural industry remain paramount. What is lost in this equation are the rights and freedom of workers. So although they participate in the paid labour force, they are accorded many fewer rights and privileges than landed immigrants or Canadian citizens.

Conclusion

This chapter shows that temporary foreign workers are on the increase in Canada. Whereas previously, labour migrants came to Canada as landed immigrants, Canada's contemporary immigration policies rely on temporary foreign workers to fill labour gaps. While some who come to Canada through this system, such as highly skilled workers, are able to benefit from these labour programs and even transition to permanent residency through the Canadian Experience Class, others, especially those who arrive through the low-skilled categories, are relegated to second-class citizenship with little control over their work or lives. Moreover, due to the ongoing temporariness of their work, they are vulnerable to abuse and exploitation with little recourse should they wish to return in future years. This inequitable organization of foreign temporary labour is creating a two-tiered system — one for highly skilled workers, who usually arrive from the U.S. or Europe, with a number of rights and privileges, including potential citizenship, and another for lower skilled workers, who often are from countries in the Global South, which is mired with controls and regulations and creates an unfree labour force.

Advocates, unions and temporary labour migrants themselves are calling on the government to make changes to foreign temporary labour programs in order to protect workers from exploitation and abuse. These changes include having better regulation and enforcement of working and housing conditions, more resources and better information distributed to temporary foreign workers so they are aware of their rights and employers' responsibilities, allowing temporary workers to transition to permanent residency and finally, changing Canada's immigration laws so low-skilled workers have the same opportunities as high-skilled workers to work, live and settle in Canada.

6. UNDER THE SURFACE
Canada's Hidden Labour Force

Undocumented migrants are a global phenomenon and the fastest growing form of migration across the world. Of this group, non-status workers make up its largest portion, presently estimated at between 30 to 40 million people, and it is calculated that undocumented workers contribute approximately $150 billion per year in global remittances.[1] Although Canada has a smaller share of undocumented migrants compared to our neighbour to the south, there has been a growing awareness of undocumented migrants working and living in Canada. But before we begin, what does the word "undocumented" mean? The definition, according to the Oxford Dictionary, is "not recorded in or proved by documents." In the context of Canada, many of the undocumented migrants who live here do have documents and have been recorded by immigration officials. In fact, it is estimated that many of Canada's so-called undocumented migrants first arrived either as refugee claimants or on tourist visas and were either denied refugee status or outstayed their visas. In some cases, immigrants have paid large sums of money (up to $50,000 per person), frequently to false agents, in order to come into Canada. Hence, they are hardly undocumented, but rather, their documents do not accord them immigrant status. Thus, we will refer to this group as non-status immigrants.

Today, it is estimated that close to 200,000 people in Canada are non-status immigrants. They are part of the Canadian cultural landscape and make up a large part of the nation's invisible labour force, working in many sectors, from cleaning to cooking to construction. Ontario's construction industry alone is said to employ over 76,000 non-status migrants, who not only provide the necessary labour to keep the industry booming but at a bargain price as well (e.g., house framers can earn up to $25 an hour, while non-status workers who are not unionized usually earn only $10). The reasons immigrants outstay their initial visas are many. For many non-status immigrants, war and violence in their home country keep them in Canada. For others, poverty and unemployment because of deteriorating economic conditions, often caused by the movement of global capital, have left them few choices for survival in their country of origin. While these reasons describe why non-status immigrants may not want to return — the "push" factors — there is another reason that keeps them here — the "pull" factor — which is Canada's need for cheap, silent labour. Non-status immigrants often work in what is called the three-D job sector — dirty, degrading and dangerous — and because of their lack of status, they are often powerless to change their working conditions. Like the temporary workers in Chapter 5, non-status immigrant workers comprise another layer of the "unfree" labour that operates in Canada.

This section of the book explores both the major issues facing non-status immigrants in Canada and some of the myths and debates surrounding non-status immigrants world-wide. Lastly, we explore how the federal government has responded to the issue of non-status immigrants and examine the community-based responses to government initiatives.

Lifestyles of the Invisible and Non-Status

> Twenty Filipinos arrived in Vancouver last May after each had paid a recruiter $5,000 plus airfare. But the factory where they were to work had burned down a month earlier. No one bothered to tell them, or to notify the government to cancel their work permits. At least two of them are now working illegally in Toronto.
>
> Tony, a 29-year-old Honduran, left his Alberta farm job after complaining of long hours and lower-than-promised wages. He rode a bus to Toronto in mid-September with two fellow Hondurans from the same farm. He now works illegally renovating homes, and his friends work illegally cleaning schools.[2]

The above events recount just two of the ways through which individuals become non-status immigrants in Canada. Contrary to the myth of being queue jumpers, many non-status immigrants arrive in Canada because of job opportunities in particular fields, often aided through intermediaries or temporary work permits. Others may have heard of hard-to-fill jobs in areas such as construction or caretaking through family members or friends in Canada. Meanwhile, high unemployment rates and/or poverty or perhaps an ongoing conflict situation will compel an individual to seek passageway into Canada either because of anticipated job prospects or the actual promise of a job through their friends and families. They may come over on a work permit, via a tourist visa or sometimes by claiming refugee status. Once in Canada, they are often hired quickly into a particular field, often located in the lower skilled sectors such as construction, agricultural work or domestic work. Part of the problem for non-status immigrants whose labour power Canadian employers are demanding is that the jobs are all located in what is called "low skilled" fields and Canada's immigration policy is geared towards rewarding status to those who have high levels of education and skill, despite labour demands and needs. Thus, if an individual such as

Tony were to apply through traditional channels, he would likely be rejected, despite the demand and need for his labour.

While in Canada and working, non-status immigrants receive less in wages than their Canadian counterparts. For example, the average wage for a unionized bricklayer is $34 an hour. Non-status immigrants usually only make half of that, sometimes even less. Because of their non-immigrant status, they cannot join unions and are also ineligible for EI benefits, vacation pay, sick days or health insurance. Despite these disadvantages and the constant risks of deportation, many non-status immigrants choose to stay and work in Canada because there is a job market for their skills. Non-status immigrants also build lives similar to status immigrants while in Canada; they have children born in Canada, they build extensive social networks, they pay taxes through their purchases, they buy houses and cars and participate in the Canadian economy just like all other Canadians. The only difference is that they do not have status and can be deported at any time. Many also attempt to regularize their immigration status while in Canada, paying thousands of dollars to costly immigration consultants who often fail at getting them the status they need to legally remain in the country. Moreover, if discovered by immigration authorities, non-status immigrants may lose everything they've earned while in Canada as authorities rush to deport them out of the country. (See the Box: The Ferreiras, which highlights an example of a family that was discovered as "illegal.")

Myths and Realities

There are a number of myths surrounding non-status immigrants and their perceived rights. This section explores some of these and examines the challenges and realities faced by non-status immigrants in light of these misperceptions.

Myth 1: Non-Status Immigrants Jump the Line

Our current immigration point system favours primarily business people with large amounts of capital, university-educated professionals who are strong in either English or French and Family Class applicants who already have family members in Canada. The majority of non-status immigrants are skilled or semi-skilled applicants who would not qualify under the point system even though there is a shortage of labour in many of their designated sectors. Given these conditions, it can be argued that technically there is no queue for them. The *Toronto Star* reported that under the new point system, most people currently living in Canada would not qualify to immigrate here.

The Ferreiras

The Ferreiras — who came to Toronto in March 1999, to visit relatives and decided to stay illegally — are typical. The children went to school, Joe worked as a bricklayer and Elizabeth got a job in a window factory. "Life was good, but we were scared to get caught," Licinio, who now works in construction, said in a weekend interview. The family had to be careful because if anyone got injured or sick, medicare wouldn't cover their hospital costs. About three years ago, at a time when rumours of an amnesty first began, they went to an immigration consultant who advised them to apply for legal status, first on humanitarian grounds and then, when that failed, as refugees. The consultant charged $4,500, the Ferreiras said. Like all refugee claims filed by Portuguese immigrants, theirs was rejected. The Ferreiras acknowledge they were here illegally and must go. But they think the policy doesn't make sense, and they don't like how they've been treated. "We're working and go to school," Licinio said. "We pay income tax, do everything by the book, but we're treated like garbage." "It's not fair, sending people home in two weeks," said cousin Paula Goncalves. "If you own a home or car, what are you supposed to do? People who work their asses off here, who aren't any trouble whatsoever, are sent home. They're hard-working people."

Source: Peter Gorrie, "Tories Begin Deporting Illegal Workers," Immigration Watch Canada, at <www.skyscrapercity.com/showthread.php?t=329484> (March 21, 2006).

Myth 2: Non-Status Immigrants Aren't Real "Immigrants," They Are Economic Migrants

Immigrants come to Canada for a variety of reasons, ranging from reuniting with family to economic pressures, from a fear of personal survival due to violence or government corruption to being able to live openly in a tolerant society that respects religious, gender and sexual diversity. Ironically, most of the first settlers in Canada could also be described as economic migrants: men and women who came from Europe in the hopes of a better life in Canada. Furthermore, the contemporary effects of corporate globalization have destroyed many rural economies and displaced millions of people due to the privatization of their economies, often from western-based multinational companies.

Myth 3: We Have Reached Our Maximum Limit of Immigrants

In reality, Canada sets its immigration targets annually at about 1 percent of the population because these immigrants are needed to sustain our economy. Canada consistently fails to meet these targets.

Myth 4: Non-Status Immigrants Are Stealing Canadian Jobs

Certain sectors of our economy are currently experiencing a shortage of skilled or semi-skilled labour, including manufacturing, construction, garment, childcare, cleaning, food, services and many others. These sectors often depend heavily on non-status immigrants to do the work that many Canadians are not interested in doing. Moreover, given their lack of status, many non-status immigrants are underpaid and exploited by their employers.

Myth 5: Non-Status Immigrants Are Criminals and Terrorists

In actuality, living without status makes one more vulnerable to crimes such as labour exploitation and sexual harassment, which non-status people are unlikely to report. Moreover, the vast majority of non-status immigrants come to Canada not to escape a criminal past but because of a promised job either through an intermediary or through social contacts. Finally, most non-status immigrants do end up working in Canada, paying taxes and being law-abiding citizens. Their only "crime" is their inability to acquire permanent residency, which by the way is not a penal crime.[3]

Here to Stay — The Systemic Reality of Non-Status Immigrants

According to the International Organization for Migration, migration is one of the defining features of the twenty-first century and is expected to increase over the next few decades. As more people across the globe face social and economic upheaval due to poverty, growing unemployment, rural dislocation, violence and internal and external conflict, more are going to seek security, safety and a better life in other countries. However, what we are currently witnessing in Canada, as well as elsewhere, is a two-tier access route to immigration. Those who have wealth, education and highly sought-out skills are able to immigrate through legal channels (although they are not always likely to find a job in their field given many employers' requirement for Canadian accreditation and experience, as shown in Chapter 3). Those who do not have the former are forced to migrate through more dubious channels, though ironically, they almost always find jobs in their fields given the high demand for semi-skilled workers. In fact, it is estimated that a non-status Mexican worker will find work within two weeks of arriving in the U.S., and a similar situation prevails in Europe, where non-status migrants are rarely "unemployed."[4] What is patently unjust in this system is that, while the needs of industry are dictating migration patterns, whether legal or illegal, only one class of immigrants receive the rights and protection of the host country. By creating a sub-class of non-status immigrants, the Canadian state is not responsible for their welfare in periods of economic downturn. As one migration expert notes, this informal sector of employment constitutes a de facto employment policy on the part of the state to meet the evolving needs of industry. Moreover, this policy of tolerance can easily be reversed in economic hard times:

> The practices of many States of tolerating the presence of migrant workers in irregular status to meet labour needs in certain sectors of the market constitutes a de facto employment policy in which part of the work force becomes a variable which can be reduced or even eliminated (in theory) in periods of economic downturn, through exercise by States of their prerogative to expel foreigners from their territory. In effect, by the same manner that migration policy can be utilized to satisfy labour market needs with foreign labour, deportation or expulsion can be utilized to regulate and even force the return to countries of origin of this temporary labour.[5]

Despite national governments' rhetoric about stemming the tide of "illegal migration," studies show that non-status migration has increased in recent years and industries world-wide are benefiting from this pool of cheap, expendable labour. For example, in Canada, middle-class families are able to hire non-status immigrants as caregivers and cleaners for a fraction of the cost they would have to pay Canadian citizens or even temporary workers, while the construction industry saves money by not having to pay union wages to non-status immigrants. Given these conditions, what are the options in dealing with non-status immigrants? The next section explores some of the policy options put forward by international bodies, non-governmental organizations and advocacy groups.

Government and Community Responses to Non-Status Immigrants

In recent years, non-status immigrants have become a hot button issue for governments, the media and a range of social organizations all around the world. Although the number of non-status immigrants in Canada is quite small, especially compared to the United States, where non-status immigrants account for roughly eight million people or about 30 percent of all the foreigners who arrive every year (it is estimated that non-status immigrants in Canada only account for 8 percent of all foreign arrivals), there is a growing concern regarding both the arrival of non-status immigrants and their living and working conditions while in Canada. In response to this phenomenon, a range of policy options has been proposed by governments, social agencies and advocacy groups. While some are awaiting adoption at various levels, others have already been implemented by local social service agencies, including schools. This section examines the different policy avenues available for government in dealing with non-status immigrants and also documents local initiatives that have been adopted by community agencies.

One of the first responses that is almost always offered when it comes to controlling the entry of non-status immigrants is to tighten the borders. Certainly, the United States has tried numerous border control tactics to restrict the entry of non-status immigrants, from constant border patrols to the building of a "Berlin Wall" like fence between the U.S. and Mexico, to strange proposals such as shaking fluorescent glow dust at the border which would tag non-status immigrants, who could later by caught be border guards using ultraviolet lights and lasers.[6] Regardless of the initiatives implemented, tens of thousands of migrants still attempt to make their way across the border every year. As one expert has noted: "the [border] crackdown has not slowed the river of humanity crossing the southwest border but has re-channeled it, [making it] more dangerous…. Migrants now die in greater numbers of thirst, hunger, sunstroke or cold. Others drown in irrigation canals."[7] Canada, unlike the United States, does not have the same border issues, but that hasn't stopped the government from implementing policies aimed at restricting the flow of people across the border.

One of the more recent policy initiatives aimed at tightening borders was the Canada–U.S. Safe Third Country Agreement, which came into effect in December 2004. This agreement was implemented as part of the U.S.–Canada Smart Border Action Plan and dictates that refugee claimants are required to request protection in the first safe country they arrive in, unless they qualify for an exception to the agreement. Critics of the agreement argue that it has the opposite effect than intended and that borders are actually made more unsafe. Prior to the agreement, refugees would present themselves at the border, get interviewed and were given a security check. Now, refugees will stop making claims and find alternate ways of crossing, including through smugglers and traffickers, as was the case in Germany when they introduced a similar plan. Moreover, many advocates argue that the U.S. is not a safe place for refugees — they are at greater risk of detention, many more are denied protection and the U.S. has a reputation for discrimination, especially against Arabs and Muslims. Lastly, Canada already accepts only one quarter of 1 percent of the world's refugee population and this agreement will only lower that number, thus putting refugees' lives at risk, both by them seeking entry through illegal channels and through the risk

Mexican Woman Deported to Her Death

A woman between the ages of 20 and 30 was found murdered – and with evidence of childbirth – with blows to her body and a bullet in the forehead, a classic revenge from drug trafficking," said a June 5 story in the Mexican newspaper *El Informador de Jalisco*. A death certificate later classified the woman's death as a homicide. What the coroner's office didn't mention was that the 24-year-old murder victim and her mother and sister had twice sought refuge in Canada, in 2004 and 2008, from drug traffickers. In 2005, their asylum claim was rejected. The board said, among other things, that the family hadn't made enough effort to seek help from Mexican authorities. Facing deportation, the family went into hiding. But in August 2008, when Grise returned to Mexico to visit her dying grandmother, she was attacked and raped, leaving her pregnant. She came back to Canada but was deported in December. Her mother and sister were deported in February. Grise was kidnapped again last March, then seven months pregnant. Her body was found in June. The death certificate determined a Caesarean section had been performed about a month before she was killed, the whereabouts of the premature baby unknown.

Source: Nicholas Keung, 2009 "Mexican Woman Deported to her Death," *Toronto Star*, at <thestar.com/news/gta/article/714781-mexican-woman-deported-to-her-death> (October 23, 2009).

may face if they are deported back to their country of origin.[8] (See the Box: Mexican Woman Deported to Her Death, which highlights the dangers encountered by failed refugee claims and why so many claimants may risk treacherous measures to get to and remain in Canada).

In addition to enacting policies that restrict border crossings, the federal government has used deportation as a way to limit the number of non-status immigrants in the country. As suggested earlier, deportation can be used as a way to regulate labour flows into country. In rising economic times, when there is an increased demand for labour, the government may turn a blind eye to non-status immigrants, who fill essential jobs in several employment sectors. However, economic downturns, a change in government or the need to court public favour may all be reasons for a shift in policy regarding non-status immigrants. For example, in 2006, the recently elected Conservative government reversed a Liberal initiative to grant status to a number of non-status immigrants who had been working and living in Canada for years. Instead, the Conservatives put increased resources into deporting thousands of non-status immigrants, many of whom were crucial to the maintenance of the construction industry. Officials went so far as to remove children of non-status immigrants from their school until parents showed up to

The Lizano-Sossa Family

Fifteen-year-old Kimberly Lizano-Sossa and her 14-year-old brother, Gerald, were pulled out of North York's Dante Alighieri Academy on April 27, 2006, the same day their mother, two-year-old Canadian-born sister and grandparents were taken into custody after police were alerted to the family's illegal status. The move came as officials attempted to draw the father out of hiding. Originally from Costa Rica, the government wanted to separate the Lizano-Sossa family by sending either the mother or father back home immediately. The family came to Canada in 2001 on a visitor visa. They then applied for refugee status, claiming they would be in danger from drug dealers if they were forced to return to their homeland. They were deported on Canada Day.

immigration authorities (see Box: The Lizano-Sossa Family). This move, which was highly criticized by the public, led to the implementation of the Don't Ask, Don't Tell (DADT) policy at the Toronto District School Board in order to protect the rights of children of non-status immigrants and their families. The DADT policy outlines that the school board would not require families or their children to divulge their immigration status. Similar policies have been adopted across Canada and in the U.S. in a range of different areas, including education and employment, in order to protect the human rights of non-status immigrants and their families.

While restricting borders and enforcing deportation orders may be a path to limiting non-status immigrants, countless studies have illustrated that these measures don't stop the flow. As long as there is the demand for labour in Canada (the "pull" factor) combined with unstable social and economic conditions in countries of origin (the "push" factor), there will be non-status immigrants in Canada. Instead, immigrant advocates and NGOs are pushing governments to recognize the inherent problems in the system and to counter the myths of non-status immigrants as "queue jumpers" and "criminals" both by amending the immigration system to allow semi-skilled people to immigrate to Canada as permanent citizens and through implementing a regularization program that gives current non-status immigrants the rights of settlement. With regard to the latter solution — regularization, this would entail granting citizenship rights to those who are living without status in Canada. Canada has implemented regularization programs in the past. From 1960–1972, the Chinese Adjustment Statement Program allowed non-status Chinese immigrants to apply for permanent residency if they could demonstrate they were of "good moral character" and were not involved in "illegal immigration." It is estimated that 12,000 people were regularized through this program. In 1973, the Adjustment of Status Program allowed approximately 39,000 people to be granted permanent residency even though the program was only active for three months. The program was geared towards immigrants who became non-status due to a change in immigration policy that no longer allowed immigrants to apply for status from within Canada. Other regularization programs included the following:

- a 1981 program that allowed 4,000 Haitians living in Quebec to regularize their status (many of whom were either political refugees or left without status because of the 1973 changes);
- the Minster's Review Committee (1983–1985), which regularized an estimated 1,000 people who were deemed to be "successfully established and integrated";
- the Deferred Removals Order Class, through which approximately 3,000 failed refugee claimants from China, Iran and other countries deemed too dangerous to deport people to were granted status; and,
- in 2002, failed refugee claimants from Algeria lobbied for and won a regularization program that saw 900 non-status Algerians granted status.

These programs demonstrate that through successful lobbying, public pressure and a sympathetic government, non-status immigrants can be granted the right to be citizens in Canada. Furthermore, as the above programs show, regularization has often come with a variety of conditions, from having "good moral character" to being "successfully integrated." Similarly, advocacy efforts around restoring regularization programs for non-status immigrants vary in their arguments with regard to the conditions for receiving status, from blanket amnesties to a minimum time period of employment. Others advocate having a two-step process, one that grants temporary work permits but then moves onto permanent citizenship. Regardless of the pathways chosen, three things are clear: non-status immigrants make a valuable and essential contribution to Canadian society through the labour they provide; no amount of border restrictions will stop the flow on non-status immigrants; and non-status immigrants and their families deserve to be treated with human dignity and respect.

Conclusion

> The product of a colonial history, today's borderlines create contradictions and tensions in an age of globalization. Increasingly, borders have been opened to capital and goods but closed to people. As a result, migrants who are forced to cross borders in order to survive have become modern outlaws.[9]

Canada has a long history with non-status immigrants. In fact, it can be argued that the first European settlers who arrived onto Canadian shores could all be considered non-status immigrants. Canada's "founding fathers" — John A. McDonald, George Brown and George Étienne-Cartier — would all qualify as undocumented migrants; men who arrived without papers and started working. According to today's policies, all three men would be eligible for deportation. But while these men were undocumented, they all did have status as citizens. Unlike the original settlers from Europe, who acquired land, rights and status upon coming to Canada in exchange for their labour power, today's non-status immigrants live as virtual prisoners with no rights and little chance of acquiring legal status despite their many years of participation in the Canadian labour force, providing labour that is vital to the Canadian economy. Non-status immigrants are the often the labourers cleaning our offices, building our homes and taking care of our children. It is estimated that as much as a quarter of the construction industry is made up of non-status immigrants, who, ironically, although employed in a dangerous industry, have no access to health care should they get injured on the job. Moreover, non-status immigrants have no recourse should they not get paid, as they cannot complain for fear of deportation.

It is these conditions that make the employment of non-status immigrants so attractive to many employers — they are a cheap, expendable labour pool that cannot complain or agitate for any human rights. Furthermore, there is no requirement to pay for Employment Insurance or the Canada Pension Plan. Similarly for the government, non-status immigrants subsidize the Canadian economy — they provide cheap labour without any long-term commitment to having to pay Employment Insurance or retirement benefits. Moreover, in times of economic recession, the government simply steps in with mass campaigns of deportation or stricter visa regulations. It is no coincidence that in 2009, in the midst of a global recession, the federal government enacted stricter tourist visa regulations for Mexican and Czech citizens.[10] However, it has been demonstrated throughout the world that despite harsher regulations and penalties for non-status immigrants, the demand for their labour continues to persist, and thus they will keep arriving. As immigration advocates argue, we need to change the immigration system so that all immigrants who contribute to the Canadian economy can benefit fully from the rights of living and working in Canada. Non-status immigrants are no exception.

7. COMING TO A BETTER PLACE?
Not Always a Happy Ending

In this concluding chapter we ask the following questions: For whom is Canada a better place? Is migrating to Canada always, or even usually, an enriching and positive experience for immigrants? In this book we show that immigration is a complex process involving individuals, institutions, employers, communities, post-secondary institutions and municipal, provincial and federal governments. It also encompasses notions of permanence and temporariness, with vastly different rights offered to people in different categories. The story of immigration to Canada is often premised on a narrative in which immigrants are improving their lives, coming to a "better place." Are they?

The history of immigration in Canada is overtly built on a particular vision of Canada, a white country based on British or French norms, languages and customs. For many years this image was made a reality through exclusionary policies and practices aimed at allowing certain people into the country and keeping other people out. Until 1967, immigration policies explicitly used notions of race for purposes of immigrant selection. With the introduction of the point system, race was eliminated as a criterion; however, by privileging education and work experience the selection system targets those deemed to be "high skilled." This class bias in our immigration system causes many problems. In order to qualify for permanent migration, an immigrant must have post-secondary education and years of relevant work experience. Those deemed as "low skilled," that is, people without post-secondary degrees, can only immigrate for permanent residency if they qualify under the Family Class. They are not eligible for citizenship if they are here through temporary work programs or as non-status workers. As temporary or non-status workers they pay taxes and work in precarious and dangerous conditions but constantly live in fear of deportation. The irony is that the "high skilled" permanent residents have such difficulty in gaining employment in their field, they often end up working side-by-side with "low skilled" temporary workers. Canada, especially in the urban centres, is becoming a country in which immigrant doctors, engineers and teachers are working in labour jobs, driving taxi cabs, cleaning office buildings and serving fast food.

Settlement services are available in each province to assist immigrants in their integration process. These services cover a wide range of employment and language based needs. Yet they are poorly funded on short-term contracts and often do not give immigrants the tools they need to integrate successfully. The funding structure of the settlement sector limits its capacity to meet the needs of immigrants. Instead of receiving core funding, settlement agencies must apply for individual grants and purchase-of-service agreements, which diverts staff time from direct service to administrative duties. Some settlement agencies offer programs to immigrants in specific professions; however, the number of immigrants who require such information and assistance may far outweigh the capacity of the programs. In addition, service agreements negotiated between the federal government and the provinces result in levels of service that differ across provincial boundaries. There is often a greater need for services, especially intermediate and longer-term services, than settlement agencies get funded to provide. The funding of settlement services needs to be treated as a "Canadian" issue, similar to education and health care, to ensure that immigrants and Canada fully realize each other's potential.

Immigrants arrive in Canada through many different channels. One of the most popular avenues to immigrate to Canada is through a temporary worker program, which as the name indicates, only provides access to immigration on a temporary basis. While some temporary work programs can be a gateway to more permanent citizenship, most are set up to ensure that Canadian industries can benefit from a cheap pool of ongoing and accessible labour that can be discarded when the season is completed or the economy experiences a downturn. Depending on the industry, many temporary immigrants who have been working in Canada for years still have no access to permanent residency. The Seasonal Agricultural Worker Program, a temporary worker program for agricultural labourers, is often touted as a model program. However, closer examination of this program reveals that many workers experience human rights abuses, including cramped and unsanitary housing and unsafe working conditions. However, workers in these programs rarely complain about conditions, as they depend on their employer for a positive evaluation in order to return the following year. These workers contribute to all of Canada's tax programs (such as income tax, Employment Insurance and the Canadian Pension Plan) and contribute to the economies of the communities they live in, yet the temporariness of their status means they receive little in the way of long-term benefits. As advocates have pointed out, if these workers are good enough to work in Canada, they are good enough to stay. More needs to be done to protect their rights and provide a path to permanent citizenship.

Our last look at immigration in Canada turns towards the underside of Canada's immigration system — non-status workers. Like many other immigrants, non-status migrants come to Canada seeking a better life for themselves and their families. They often travel here under specific work programs or because of the promise of work from social contacts in Canada. However, unlike permanent residents or temporary workers, non-status migrants have neither legal status nor rights in Canada. Despite the fact that many industries, from construction to hospitality to caretaking, rely heavily on the labour of non-status workers, Canada's immigration point system is designed to exclude these workers. Scholars and advocates point out that while national economies depend on the labour of non-status migrants to keep labour costs low in good economic times, during an economic recession, these same governments initiate deportation programs to rid themselves of "excess immigrants." But all immigrants deserve to be treated with dignity and respect, and similarly to temporary workers, if non-status immigrants are good enough to work, they are good enough to stay.

Land of Opportunity or Depot of Dumped Labour?

Canada prides itself on being a multicultural nation. We stand on the global stage and promote tolerance, diversity and acceptance. We are known for having one of the most generous immigration policies in the world. Yet, if we dig beneath the surface of this rosy image, we see cracks in our claims. Certainly, our multicultural nation was not built through the benevolence and generosity of previous governments but through carefully calculated labour and immigration policies that imported different "races" of immigrants for specific tasks – railroad construction, childcare, agricultural work, nursing.

Our contemporary immigration policies, although not as explicitly racist as their predecessors, continue to stratify immigrants according to the nation's labour demands and governments' political agendas. Much of Canada's need for labour lies in the low-skilled sectors of employment, yet these are not the immigrants Canada welcomes into its notion of citizenship and nationhood. So these labourers remain temporary, or worse, non-status, easily expendable once their labour is no longer needed. On the other side, Canada imports highly trained professionals with the promise of jobs, citizenship and the opportunity for a better life, yet less than one in four of these migrants obtain work in their field and they are less likely to be employed than native-born Canadians.[1] An interesting fact about this group is that their children are likely to follow in their parents' professional footsteps. As a recent government memo revealed about these children, "Chinese and South Asian are the most likely to have university degrees or higher, and to be employed in high-skilled occupations,"[2] while children of Caribbean and Latin American origin tend not to fare so well. They often have lower levels of education than Canadian-born and end up in lower-skilled jobs. Interestingly, Asian immigration has been on the rise since 1999, while Caribbean immigration levels have been drastically reduced. On the other hand, many of the low-skilled temporary work programs are targeted to Caribbean and Latin American migrants. It is no coincidence that Canada's immigration policy is predicated on explicitly creating a nation where people with only a specified type of skill, education and experience are valued, while everyone else needed to keep the nation functioning is kept marginal and deprived of the nation's rights and citizenship.

Immigration is a critical issue for Canada, a large geographic country with an aging population, a diverse citizenry and a low birth rate. There are many reasons — from economic to social — why immigration is imperative. We need immigration to fill labour market shortages, to stimulate the economy, to advance our knowledge and understanding of science, medicine and human societies, to reunite families, to help people in dangerous situations and to build strong communities. We have to examine our immigration policies and practices carefully in order to ensure that they are fair, effective, transparent, democratic and comprehensive. Immigration needs to be seen as the entire process from application to integration, and for this to work effectively all levels of government need to coordinate their efforts. Our national immigration strategy has to work in conjunction with relevant employment and settlement strategies to ensure that immigrants do not have to face unnecessary obstacles and time-consuming delays to the process of settling in their new home and to putting their skills into practice in the labour market. It is at our peril that we ignore the urgent challenges that Canada faces in its immigration strategy. The recent shifts in world migration due to the growing strength of the Chinese and Indian economies are having an impact on the global competition for new citizens and workers. Unless Canada ensures that all immigrants are given the opportunity to participate fully in society and according to their abilities, Canada will not only lose those immigrants who have experienced unfavourable labour market access, but will also fail to attract new migrants. There is a also a serious need to review the temporary worker policies, which bring in more immigrants each year than the traditional immigration policies and are creating an ever-growing pool of dispensable labour. Both our ability to compete in the global economies and our reputation as a humanitarian country that welcomes the world's citizens are on the line.

ENDNOTES

Introduction: Immigration: A Critical Analysis

1. International Organization for Migration, "Facts and Figures," at <iom.int/jahia/Jahia/lang/en/pid/241>, (n.d.).
2. International Organization for Migration, "World Migration 2008: Managing Labour Mobility in the Evolving Global Economy: Regional and Country Figures," at <iom.int/jahia/Jahia/about-migration/facts-and-figures/regional-and-country-figures>. (n.d.).
3. United Way of Calgary and Area, "Five Myths about Immigrants," at <aaisa.ca/files/Five percent20Myths percent20Abouth percent20Immigrants percent20-percent20United percent20Way.pdf> (2009).
4. United Way of Calgary and Area, "Five Myths about Immigrants."
5. Peter Stalker, *The No-Nonsense Guide to International Migration* (Toronto, Between the Lines Press, 2008; and Saskia Sassen, *Globalization and its Discontents* (New York: New Press, 1998).

Chapter One: The Evolution of Immigration Policy

1. *Canadian Encyclopedia*, "Immigration" (Toronto: McClelland & Stewart, 1999), p. 1139.
2. Irving Abella and Harold Troper, *None Is Too Many: Canada and the Jews of Europe 1933–1948,* Third Edition. (Toronto: Lester Publishing, 1991).
3. Santayana, George, *The Life of Reason* Volume 1 (New York: Prometheus Press, 1905).
4. Irving Abella, "Foreword," in B. Roberts, *Whence They Came: Deportations from Canada 1900–1935* (Ottawa: University of Ottawa Press, 1988) p. vii.

5. Citizenship and Immigration Canada, "Growing Together: A Backgrounder on Immigration and Citizenship" (Ottawa: Author, 1995) p. 2.
6. The apology read: Be it resolved that this Legislature apologizes for the events of May 23, 1914, when 376 passengers of the *Komagata Maru*, stationed off Vancouver harbour, were denied entry by Canada. The House deeply regrets that the passengers who sought refuge in our country and our province were turned away without benefit of the fair and impartial treatment befitting a society where people of all cultures are welcomed and accepted.
7. Adele Perry, "White Women, Race and Immigration to British Columbia," in M. Epp, F. Iacovetta, F. Swyripa (eds.), *Sisters or Strangers? Immigrant, Ethnic and Racialized Women in Canadian History* (Toronto: University of Toronto Press, 2004).
8. "Move to Check Smuggling of Chinese into Canada," *Toronto Daily News* (January 24, 1913).
9. Guida Man, "Racism, Sexism and the Experience of Chinese Immigrant Women," at <http://web.archive.org/web/20051027021558re_/geog.queensu.ca/era21/papers/man.htm> (2000).
10. Valerie Knowles, *Forging Our Legacy: Canadian Citizenship and Immigration 1900–1977.* (Ottawa: Public Works and Government Services Canada, 2000).
11. Christiane Harzig, "MacNamara's DP Domestics: Immigration Policy Makers Negotiate Class, Race, and Gender in the Aftermath of World War II," *Social Politics: International Studies in Gender, State & Society* 10 (2003).
12. "Action on British Immigration," *Saturday Night* (December 29, 1928) p. 4.
13. W. Marchington, "Migration Left to Provinces Which Will Decide Own Needs Under New Policy of Ottawa," *The Globe* (March 5, 1930) p. 1.
14. W. Baldwin, "Mackenzie King Encourages Immigration for Growth," *Globe and Mail* (May 2, 1947) p. 1.
15. W. Baldwin, "Mackenzie King," p. 2.
16. Harold Troper, "History of Immigration to Toronto Since the Second World War: From Toronto 'the Good' to Toronto 'the World in a City'," at <ceris.metropolis.net/frameset_e.html> (2000) p. 7.
17. Statistics Canada, "100 Years of Education," *Education Quarterly Review* 7,3 (2001).
18. W. MacEachern, "Ottawa Eases Color Bar on Immigration," *Toronto Daily Star* (January 20, 1962).

19. Counselling Foundation of Canada, "A Coming of Age: Counselling Canadians for Work in the Twentieth Century" (Toronto: Author, 2002) p. 57.
20. Statistics Canada, "The Daily: 2006 Census: Ethnic Origin, Visible Minorities, Place of Work and Mode of Transportation," at <http://www12.statcan.gc.ca/census-recensement/2006/rt-td/eth-eng.cfm> (2008); and Statistics Canada, *Canada's Ethnocultural Mosaic, 2006 Census* (Ottawa: Ministry of Industry, 2008).
21. Statistics Canada, *The Canadian Immigrant Labour Market in 2006: First Results from Canada's Labour Force Survey* (Ottawa: Ministry of Industry, 2007).
22. Grace Edward Galabuzi, *Canada's Economic Apartheid: The Social Exclusion of Racialized Groups in the New Century* (Toronto: Canadian Scholars' Press, 2006).

Chapter Two: Immigration Policy and Practices

1. Government of Canada, "Minister of Citizenship and Immigration Canada Heading to India," at <canadavisa.com/minister-of-citizenship-and-immigration-canada-heading-to-india-071022.html> (2007).
2. Peter Stalker, *The No-Nonsense Guide to International Migration* (Toronto: Between the Lines Press, 2008).
3. 0 = Managerial; Skill Level A are those occupations that usually require university education; Skill Level B are occupations that usually require community college or skilled apprenticeship.
4. Other conditions apply. You cannot be sponsored as a spouse, a common-law partner or a conjugal partner if (a) you (or your sponsor) were married to someone else at the time of your marriage; (b) you have lived apart from your sponsor for at least one year and either you (or your sponsor) are the common-law or conjugal partner of another person; (c) your sponsor immigrated to Canada and, at the time they applied for permanent residence, you were a family member who should have been examined to see if you met immigration requirements, but you were not examined; or (d) the sponsor previously sponsored another spouse, common-law partner or conjugal partner, and three years have not passed since that person became a permanent resident.
5. At the time of writing, the government of the day has proposed significant reforms to the refugee policy, specifically the appeal process at the Immigration and Review Board and the process for applications from "safe" countries.
6. Canadian Council for Refugees, 2005, "An Overview of Canada's

Refugee Policy," at <ccrweb.ca/refpolicy.ppt>.
7. Peter Showler, "Refugee Forum: From Immigration and Integration," at <maytree.com/policyPDF/PolicyInsights2010RefugeeForum.pdf> (2010).
8. See <http://chaudhrysolidarity.wordpress.com/>.

Chapter Three:. Immigrants and the Labour Market

1. Daily Bread Food Bank, "Who's Hungry?" at <dailybread.ca/get_informed/upload/WH-08-STATS2.pdf> (2008).
2. Eleonore Kofman, "Female Birds of Passage a Decade Later: Gender and Immigration in the European Union," *International Migration Review* 33 (1999).
3. Statistics Canada, "Longitudinal Survey of Immigrants to Canada," at <statcan.ca/Daily/English/030904/d030904a.htm> (2003).
4. Danielle Zeitsma, "Immigrants Working in Regulated Professions," *Perspectives* (February 2010), at <statcan.gc.ca/pub/75-001-x/2010102/pdf/11121-eng.pdf>.
5. Nixon in Madelaine Drohan and Matthew Sherwood, "Not Left Behind: How Canada Can Compete: A Discussion Paper from the Economist Intelligence Unit," at <accenture.com/NR/rdonlyres/09E9B1E2-E839-4DEC-88EA-9E8A270C7685/0/Canadacombo.pdf> (2007) p. 12.
6. Valerie Preston, Nina Damsbaek, Philip Kelly, Maryse Lemoine, Lucia Lo, John Shields and Steven Tufts, "What Are the Labour Market Outcomes for University-Educated Immigrants?" at <yorku.ca/tiedi/doc/AnalyticalReport4.pdf> (2010).
7. Rosalie Abella, *Equality in Employment: A Royal Commission Report* (Ottawa: Minister of Supply and Services Canada, 1984) p. v.
8. Rosalie Abella, *Equality in Employment*, p. 50.
9. P. Cumming, E. Lee, and D.G. Oreopoulos, *Access: Task Force on Access to Professions and Trades in Ontario* (Toronto: Ontario Ministry of Citizenship, 1989).
10. P. Cumming et al., *Access*, p. xi.
11. Canadian Business Resource Centre and the Canadian Centre for Women's Education and Development, *The Economic Integration of Immigrant Women in Toronto: A Bilateral Perspective, Second Edition,* at <cbrc.com/paper.html> (2002).
12. Ontario Ministry of Training, Colleges and Universities, *The Facts Are In! A Study of the Characteristics of Immigrants Seeking Employment in Regulated Professions in Ontario* (Toronto: Queen's Printer for Ontario, 2002).

128　ABOUT CANADA: IMMIGRATION

13. Public Policy Forum, *Bringing Employers into the Immigration Debate: Survey and Conference* (Ottawa, Public Policy Forum, 2004) p. i.
14. Public Policy Forum, *Bringing Employers*, p. 4.
15. Jeffrey Reitz, "Tapping Immigrants' Skills," *Choices* 11, 1 (2005) p. 5.
16. Rosalie Abella, *Equality in Employment*, p. 49–50.
17. Rosalie Abella, *Equality in Employment*, p. 269.
18. Policy Roundtable Mobilizing Professions and Trades, "In the Public Interest: Immigrant Access to Regulated Professions in Today's Ontario" (Toronto: Author, 2004) p. 65.
19. Bonnie Slade, "Engineering Barriers: An Empirical Investigation into the Mechanics of Downward Mobility," *Socialist Studies* 4, 2 (2008) p. 21–40.
20. Jane Cullingworth and Gurmeet Bambrah, "Access to Experience," *Engineering Dimension* (March/April, 2004).
21. Sarah Wayland, 2006, "Unsettled: Legal and Policy Barriers for Newcomers to Canada: Literature Review," Law Commission of Canada and Community Foundations of Canada.
22. Daniel Schugurensky and Bonnie Slade, "New Immigrants, Volunteer Work and Labour Market Integration: On Learning and Re-building Social Capital," in D. Livingstone, P. Sawchuk and K. Mirchandani (eds.), *The Future of Lifelong Learning and Work: Critical Perspectives* (Rotterdam: Sense Publishers, 2008).
23. Carol Goar, "Immigrant Dream Turning Sour," *Toronto Star* (July 25, 2007) p. A6.
24. Conference Board of Canada, "How Canada Performs: A Report Card on Canada," at <sso.conferenceboard.ca/e-library/LayoutAbstract.asp?DID=2047> (2007) p. 19.

Chapter Four: The Reception Party

1. Ratna Omidvar and Ted Richmond, "Immigrant Settlement and Social Inclusion in Canada" (Toronto: Laidlaw Foundation 2003).
2. Ratna Omidvar and Ted Richmond, "Immigrant Settlement."
3. Sarah Wayland, "Unsettled: Legal and Policy Barriers for Newcomers to Canada: Literature Review," Law Commission of Canada and Community Foundations of Canada (2006).
4. Citizenship and Immigration Canada, "A Commitment to Foreign Credential Recognition: Government of Canada Progress Report 2009," at <http://www.credentials.gc.ca/about/pdf/progress-report2009.pdf> (2009).
5. Sarah Wayland, "Unsettled."

6. Sarah Wayland, "Unsettled."
7. W.Y. Beyene, "Settlement Service Needs for Ethiopian Newcomers in Toronto" (Toronto: Ethiopian Association in Toronto, 2000).
8. Kareem Sadiq, "The Two-Tier Settlement System: A Review of Current Newcomer Settlement Services in Canada," at <ceris.metropolis.net/Virtual%20Library/other/CWP34_Sadiq.pdf> (2004).
9. Kareem Sadiq, "The Two-Tier Settlement System."
10. Kareem Sadiq, "The Two-Tier Settlement System."

Chapter Five: The Revolving Door

1. Citizenship and Immigration Canada, "Facts and Figures: Immigration Overview Permanent and Temporary Residents," at <cic.gc.ca/english/resources/statistics/facts2007/glossary.asp> (2007).
2. Citizenship and Immigration Canada, "Annual Report to Parliament on Immigration, 2009," at <http://www.cic.gc.ca/english/resources/publications/annual-report2009/section2.asp> (n.d.).
3. Human Resources and Skills Development Canada, "Steps to Hire Temporary Foreign Workers," at <http://www.rhdcc-hrsdc.gc.ca/eng/workplaceskills/foreign_workers/temp_workers.shtml> (2009).
4. Nicola C. Armacost, "Gender and Immigration Law: The Recruitment of Domestic Workers to Canada, 1867–1940," *Indian Journal of Gender Studies* 2 (March, 1995).
5. Ninette Kelly and Michael Trebilcock, *The Making of the Mosaic: A History of Canadian Immigration Policy* (Toronto, Ontario: University of Toronto Press, 1998).
6. Nicola C. Armacost, "Gender and Immigration Law."
7. A. Macklin, "Foreign Domestic Worker: Surrogate Housewife or Mail Order Servant?" *McGill Law Journal* 37 (1992).
8. Nandita Sharma, *Home Economics: Nationalism and the Making of Migrant Workers in Canada* (Toronto: University of Toronto Press, 2006).
9. Given the average profile of most migrant workers (i.e., low levels of education, language ability and accompanying large families), the maximum point allotment most workers would obtain in taking the assessment would be 33, far short of the minimum 67 points reuired for consideration. Moreover, within the National Occupation List, which defines employment areas in Canada that require skilled workers, agricultural work appears only in the category of inspectors, managers, specialists or consultants.
10. T. Basok, *Tortillas and Tomatoes: Transmigrant Mexican Harvesters in Canada*

(Montreal: McGill-Queen's University Press, 2002).
11. The temporary foreign workers coming from the United States include highly skilled workers.
12. Citizenship and Immigration Canada, "Facts and Figures 2008 – Immigration Overview: Permanent and Temporary Residents" at <http://www.cic.gc.ca/english/resources/statistics/facts2008/temporary/03.asp>.
13. United Food and Commercial Workers Union, "The Status of Migrant Farm Workers in Canada: 2008–2009," at <ufcw.ca/Theme/UFCW/files/PDF%202009/2009ReportEN.pdf> (2009).
14. Human Resources and Skills Development Canada, "Temporary Foreign Worker Program: Labour Market Opinion (LMO) Statistics." At <http://www.hrsdc.gc.ca/eng/workplaceskills/foreign_workers/stats/quarterly/table7q.shtml> (2009).
15. T. Basok, *Tortillas and Tomatoes*.
16. T. Basok, "Migration of Mexican Seasonal Farm Workers to Canada and Development: Obstacles to Productive Investment," *International Migration Review* 34, 1 (2000).
17. T. Basok, "He came, He Saw, He… Stayed. Guest Worker Programmes and the Issue of Non-Return," *International Migration* 38, 2 (2000).
18. T. Basok, *Tortillas and Tomatoes*.
19. T. Basok, *Tortillas and Tomatoes*.
20. M.S. Lee, *El Contrato*, video (Canada: National Film Board, 2003).
21. Nupur Gogia, "Mobile Corridors: Unpacking the Global Voyages of Labour and Leisure" (unpublished doctoral dissertation, University of Toronto, 2007).
22. Agricultural Workers Alliance, "Guatemalan Migrant Workers Deserve Our Respect," at <http://awa-ata-blog.blogspot.com/2010_07_01_archive.html> (n.d.).

Chapter Six: Under the Surface

1. L. Magalhaes, C. Carrasco and D. Gastaldo, "Undocumented Migrants in Canada: A Scope Literature Review on Health, Access to Services, and Working Conditions," *Immigrant Minority Health* 12 (2010).
2. S. Contenta and R. Monsebraaten, "How We're Creating an Illegal Workforce," *Toronto Star*, at <thestar.com/news/investigations/article/719355--how-we-re-creating-an-illegal-workforce> (November 9, 2009).
3. No One Is Illegal, "Regularization — Status for All," at <noii-van.resist.

ca/?page_id=89> (n.d.).
4. P. Taran and E. Geronimi, "Globalization, Labour and Migration: Protection Is Paramount," at <ilo.org/public/english/protection/migrant/download/pom/pom3e.pdf> (International Labour Office, n.d.).
5. P. Taran and E. Geronimi, "Globalization, Labour and Migration" p. 6.
6. Helen Hayes, *U.S. Immigration Policy and the Undocumented: Ambivalent Laws, Furtive Lives* (Westport, CT: Praegar, 2001).
7. Dillon, in Helen Hayes, *U.S. Immigration Policy* p. 131.
8. Canadian Council for Refugees, "10 Good Reasons Why Safe Third Country Is a Bad Deal," at <ccrweb.ca//10reasons.html> (n.d.).
9. M.S. Lee, "Borderless," video (Canada, 2006).
10. In 2009, the immigration minister regulated that citizens from Mexico and the Czech Republic would now require tourist visas for a visit to Canada. The government argued that these visas would stem the number of refugee claimants from these two countries, which was "creating significant delays and spiraling new costs in our refugee program" (Citizenship and Immigration Canada, "Canada Imposes a Visa on Mexico," at <cic.gc.ca/english/department/media/releases/2009/2009-07-13.asp> 2009). Canadian citizens do not require tourist visas for either Mexico or the Czech Republic.

Chapter Seven: Coming to a Better Place?

1. Danielle Zeitsma, "Immigrants Working in Regulated Professions," *Perspectives*, at <statcan.gc.ca/pub/75-001-x/2010102/pdf/11121-eng.pdf> (February 2010).
2. Charlie Gillis, "Who Doesn't get into Canada," *Maclean's Magazine* at <http://www2.macleans.ca/2010/06/17/who-doesnt-get-into-canada> (June 17, 2010).

RESOURCES

We encourage you to continue learning more about immigration policy, labour market issues, temporary work programs, immigrant settlement services and undocumented workers. What is your migration story? When did your family come to Canada and under what circumstances? Learning about immigration is a way to learn more about ourselves. We suggest the following resources as a starting point.

Chapter One: Evolution of Immigration Policy
- *The Book of Negroes* by Lawrence Hill tells the story of the Black Loyalists in Canada <http://www.lawrencehill.com/the_book_of_negroes.html>.
- Canadian Chinese National Council (CCNC) is an advocacy group with a mandate to promote the rights of all individuals, in particular those of Chinese Canadians, and to encourage their full and equal participation in Canadian society <www.ccnc.ca>.
- Komagata Maru: There is much written about this incident, in addition to films. We encourage you to check out <http://www.komagatamaru.ca/index.asp>.

Chapter Two: Immigration Policy and Practices
- Mahar Arar's website: check out <http://www.maherarar.ca/> for more detail.

- UN Declaration of Human Rights: On December 10, 1948, the General Assembly of the United Nations adopted and proclaimed the Universal Declaration of Human Rights. The full text of the document is here <http://www.un.org/en/documents/udhr/index.shtml>.
- Canadian Council for Refugees: The Canadian Council for Refugees is a non-profit umbrella organization committed to the rights and protection of refugees in Canada and around the world and to the settlement of refugees and immigrants in Canada <http://www.ccrweb.ca/eng/engfront/frontpage.htm>.

Chapter Three: Immigrants and the Labour Market

- The Maytree Foundation is a private Canadian charitable foundation established in 1982, committed to reducing poverty and inequality in Canada and to building strong civic communities <maytree.com>.
- The Council of Agencies Serving South Asians is a social justice umbrella organization working with Ontario's diverse South Asian communities. There are links here to PROMPT and Capacity Canada, a national initiative aiming to reduce labour market barriers for immigrants <http://www.cassaonline.com/index3/>.
- The Council for Access to the Profession of Engineering is a member-based organization run by and for internationally educated engineers <http://www.capeinfo.ca>.
- The Toronto Immigrant Employment Data Initiative seeks to assist community organizations whose mandate includes the better integration of immigrants into Toronto's labour force. Located at York University, this research centre has produced clear and focused research that is useful for people interested in immigration issues <http://www.yorku.ca/tiedi/index.html>.
- Workers' Action Centre is a worker-based organization committed to improving the lives and working conditions of workers in

low-wage and precarious employment <www.workersactioncentre.org>.

Chapter Four: The Reception Party

- Citizenship and Immigration Canada: Welcome to Canada — A list of settlement agencies across Canada <http://www.cic.gc.ca/english/resources/publications/welcome/wel-20e.asp>.
- Metropolis Canada is an international network for comparative research and public policy development on migration, diversity and immigrant integration in cities in Canada and around the world <http://canada.metropolis.net/>.
- CERIS-Metropolis is a research knowledge creation and transfer network that focuses on the resettlement and integration of immigrants and refugees in Ontario <http://ceris.metropolis.net>.

Chapter Five: The Revolving Door

- Justice for Migrant Workers is an advocacy group for temporary workers <http://www.justicia4migrantworkers.org/>.
- *El Contrato* by Min-Sook Lee is a chilling documentary that looks at the Mexican Seasonal Agricultural Worker Program. Available through the National Film Board of Canada <http://www.nfb.ca/film/el_contrato>.
- The Toronto Organization for Domestic Workers' Rights (Intercede) is an advocacy organization that works with live-in caregivers located in Toronto <www.intercedetoronto.org>.
- The West Coast Domestic Workers' Association is an advocacy organization that works with live-in caregivers located on the west coast <http://www.wcdwa.ca/>.
- United Food and Commercial Workers Union has been organizing to unionize temporary agricultural workers across Canada <http://www.ufcw.ca/>.

Chapter Six: Under the Surface
- No One is Illegal is an advocacy group that rallies on behalf on non-status migrants, with chapters in Montreal, Ottawa, Toronto and Vancouver <http://www.nooneisillegal.org/>.
- Status Campaign is a broad coalition of individuals and organizations advocating for the regularization of status of all non-status immigrants in Canada <http://www.ocasi.org/status/index.asp>.
- *Borderless* is a film by Min-Sook Lee about non-status immigrants in Canada. Available through Kairos <www.kairoscanada.org>.

Appendix 1

Top Source Countries of Immigrants 1968–2008

Year	#1	Number	#2	Number
1968	Britain	39,434	United States	20,422
1969	Britain	33,212	United States	22,785
1970	Britain	27,620	United States	24,424
1971	United States	24,366	Britain	15,451
1972	United States	22,618	Britain	18,197
1973	Britain	26,973	United States	25,242
1974	Britain	38,456	United States	26,541
1975	Britain	34,978	United States	20,155
1976	Britain	21,548	United States	17,315
1977	Britain	17,977	United States	12,888
1978	Britain	11,801	United States	9,945
1979	Vietnam	19,859	Britain	12,853
1980	Vietnam	25,541	Britain	18,245
1981	Britain	21,154	United States	10,559
1982	Britain	16,445	United States	9,360
1983	United States	7,381	India	7,041
1984	Vietnam	10,950	Hong Kong	7,696
1985	Vietnam	10,404	Hong Kong	7,380

Year	#1	Number	#2	Number
1986	United States	7,275	India	6,940
1987	Hong Kong	16,170	India	9,692
1988	Hong Kong	23,281	India	10,409
1989	Hong Kong	19,908	Poland	15,985
1990	Hong Kong	29,261	Poland	16,579
1991	Hong Kong	22,340	Poland	15,731
1992	Hong Kong	38,910	Philippines	13,273
1993	Hong Kong	36,574	India	20,472
1994	Hong Kong	44,169	Philippines	19,097
1995	Hong Kong	31,746	India	16,215
1996	Hong Kong	29,988	India	21,291
1997	Hong Kong	22,250	India	19,615
1998	China	19,789	India	15,376
1999	China	29,138	India	17,452
2000	China	36,746	India	26,126
2001	China	40,363	India	27,906
2002	China	33,294	India	28,838
2003	China	36,236	India	24,589
2004	China	36,411	India	25,569
2005	China	42,292	India	33,146
2006	China	33,079	India	30,754
2007	China	27,013	India	26,052
2008	China	29,336	India	24,549

Appendix 2

Federal Skilled Worker Assessment Test

1. Education (25 points)

Highest Level of Education	Points
Did not complete secondary school	0
Obtained a secondary school credential	5
Obtained a one-year diploma, trade certificate or apprenticeship and completed at least 12 years of full-time or full-time equivalent studies	12
Obtained a one-year diploma, trade certificate or apprenticeship and completed at least 13 years of full-time or full-time equivalent studies; or obtained a one-year university degree at the bachelor's level and completed at least 13 years of full-time or full-time equivalent studies	15
Obtained a two-year diploma, trade certificate or apprenticeship and completed at least 14 years of full-time or full-time equivalent studies; or obtained a university degree of two years or more at the bachelor's level and completed at least 14 years of full-time or full-time equivalent studies	20

Obtained a three-year diploma, trade certificate or apprenticeship (other than university) and completed at least 15 years of full-time or full-time equivalent studies; or Obtained two or more university degrees at the bachelor's level and completed at least 15 years of full-time or full-time equivalent studies	22
Obtained a master's or Ph.D. and completed at least 17 years of full-time education or full-time equivalent studies	25

2. English and French language ability (maximum 24 points)

To assess your English and French ability, first decide which language you are most comfortable with. This language is your first official language. The language you feel less comfortable communicating in is your second official language.

	First Official Language (16 points)				**Second Official Language** (8 points)			
Proficiency	High	Moderate	Basic	None	High	Moderate	Basic	None
Read	4	2	1	0	2	2	1	0
Write	4	2	1	0	2	2	1	0
Speak	4	2	1	0	2	2	1	0
Listen	4	2	1	0	2	2	1	0

3. Work Experience (21 points)

You must have at least one year of full-time paid work experience, or the equivalent in part-time work, in an occupation listed in the National Occupational Classification (NOC) list. Your experience must be listed in an occupation listed in Skill Type 0 or Skill Levels A or B of the NOC and it must have occurred in the past 10 years. You must have performed most of the duties, including all the essential duties that are listed for the occupation.

Work Experience	Points
Less than 1 year	0
More than 1 year but less than 2 years	15
More than 2 years but less than 3 years	17
More than 3 years but less than 4 years	19
4 or more years	21

4. Age (10 points)

Age	Points
Less than 17, or over 53	0
17	2
18	4
19	6
20	8
21–49	10
50	8
51	6
52	4
53	2

5. Arranged Employment (maximum 10 points)

To obtain points for this factor, you must have a permanent job offer in Canada, be capable of carrying out the work, and likely to accept the job. The job offer must be in an occupation listed in Skill Type 0 or Skill Level A or B of the National Occupational Classification. One of the following situations must also apply.

Arranged Employment?	Points
No	0
Yes	10

6. Adaptability (maximum 10 points)

	Points
Principal applicant's spouse/partner did not complete secondary school	0
Principal applicant's spouse/partner obtained a one-year diploma, trade certificate or apprenticeship and completed at least 12 years of full-time or full-time equivalent studies; or a one-year diploma, trade certificate or apprenticeship or university degree at the bachelor's level and completed at least 13 years of full-time or full-time equivalent studies	3
Principal applicant's spouse/partner obtained a two-year diploma, trade certificate or apprenticeship or university degree at the bachelor's level and completed at least 14 years of full-time or full-time equivalent studies; or obtained a three-year diploma, trade certificate or apprenticeship (other than university) and completed at least 15 years of full-time or full-time equivalent studies; or obtained two or more university degrees at the bachelor's level and completed at least 15 years of full-time or full-time equivalent studies	4
Principal applicant's spouse/partner obtained a master's or Ph.D. and completed at least 17 years of full-time education or full-time equivalent studies	5
Principal applicant or the spouse/partner has completed at least two years of post-secondary education in Canada since the age of 17	5

	Points
Principal applicant or the spouse/partner has completed at least one year of full-time work in Canada since the age of 17	5
Principal applicant has arranged employment in Canada	5
Principal applicant or spouse/partner has family in Canada (parent, grandparent, aunt, uncle, sister, brother, niece, nephew, child or grandchild, spouse or common-law partner who is a Canadian citizen or permanent resident living in Canada)	5

ACKNOWLEDGEMENTS

This book has been an important project for both of us. We would like to thank Fernwood Publishing, in particular Errol Sharpe for his encouragement, support and commitment to social justice; Candida Hadley for her insightful feedback; and Brenda Conroy, Debbie Mathers and Beverley Rach for their expertise in pulling it all together.

We also deeply appreciate the generous support of Anju Gogia and Jane Cullingworth, who read the first fully completed draft of the manuscript and provided feedback that improved the book immensely. Bonnie would like to thank Jane Cullingworth for her constant support, keen editorial eye and wealth of knowledge on these issues that are also so close to her heart. Bonnie would also like to thank Terry Kehoe for his sustained interest and encouragement.

It is our hope that this book will increase awareness of the difficulties encountered by both permanent and temporary migrants in Canada. Canada is recognized as a leader in formal human rights legislation, and we need to ensure that the intent of these progressive documents becomes a lived reality for everyone.

ABOUT CANADA

From health care to agriculture, childcare, globalization, immigration, energy, water and more: the books in this series explore key issues for Canadians. About Canada books provide basic — but critical and passionate — coverage of central aspects of our society. Written in accessible language by experts in their fields, the books are presented in a popular format, at affordable prices.